THE
LAKE
POETS

THE
LAKE
POETS

GAVIN D. SMITH

AMBERLEY

For Ruth

First published 2010

Amberley Publishing
Cirencester Road, Chalford,
Stroud, Gloucestershire, GL6 8PE

www.amberley-books.com

Copyright © Gavin D. Smith, 2010
The right of Gavin D. Smith to be identified as the
Author of this work has been asserted in accordance with the Copyrights,
Designs and Patents Act 1988.

All photographs Copyright © Ed Geldard

British Library Cataloguing in Publication Data.
A catalogue record for this book is available from the British Library.

ISBN 978 1 84868 536 9

Typesetting and origination by Amberley Publishing
Printed in Great Britain

Contents

Preface

I have extended the membership of the 'school' of Lake Poets to include Wordsworth's sister Dorothy, Coleridge's son Hartley, and Thomas de Quincey, and the order in which the writers are treated reflects the order in which they moved to the Lake District.

Apart from giving an overall view of the Lake Poets and their work, one aim of this book is to provide an opportunity for readers to discover more about writers like Southey and Hartley Coleridge, who have been neglected in recent years, and whose writing is frequently difficult to find in print.

Steamboats on Windermere

Introduction

The term 'Lake Poets' was first coined in 1801 by Francis Jeffrey, editor of the recently-founded *Edinburgh Review*. Writing about Robert Southey's epic poem *Thalaba The Destroyer*, Jeffrey complained that it lacked originality, and proceeded to attack what he called '... this new school of Lake Poets,' in which he included Southey, Wordsworth and Coleridge, a 'mischievous fraternity' who lived on the '... squashy banks of a lake ... debasing those feelings which poetry is designed to communicate.'

The impression, as with any 'school' in art or literature, is of a group of like-minded individuals, who share certain common beliefs, yet the 'Lake Poets' were principally connected by geography. Thomas de Quincey wrote in 1834 that '... the critics of the day, unaware of the real facts, supposed them to have assembled under common views in literature – particularly with regard to the true theory of poetic diction. Under this original blunder, laughable it is to mention, that they went on to find in their writings all the agreements and common characteristics which their blunder had presumed; and they incorporated the whole community under the name of the Lake School. Yet Wordsworth and Southey never had one principle in common.'

Byron was one of the most outspoken critics of the Lake Poets, and in the Dedication to *Don Juan* he wrote:

> You gentlemen, by dint of long seclusion
>   From better company, have kept your own
> At Keswick, and through still continued fusion
>   Of one another's minds at last have grown
> To deem, as a most logical conclusion,
>   That poesy has wreaths for you alone.
> There is a narrowness in such a notion,
>   Which makes me wish you'd change your lakes for ocean.

Blea Tarn
Described by Wordsworth as 'a liquid pool that glittered in the sun'.

The Original Three Shires Stones
The original Three Shires Stones that stood at the head of the Wrynose Pass.

The latter-day Lake Poet Norman Nicholson said of his predecessors: 'They were not indigenous. They were never acclimatised, they never really established themselves. They caught and flourished for a while like the seeds of an exotic plant brought accidentally in the packing-straw of a merchant steamer. Then, after a prodigious season, they withered and died. They remained always separate, alien, self-conscious ...'

'There is something false about the very term "Lake Poet",' continued Nicholson. 'It began as a sneer, and it has ended as a vague proprietary title, a trademark, by which certain writers attain the rank of local worthies without one's needing to read them.'

Castle Rigg Circle (Winter)
The poet John Keats visited Castle Rigg in 1882 as part of his major walking tour of Britain. He was to immortalise it in Book II of *Hyperion* with the words, 'like a dismal cirque of Druid stones, upon a forlorn moor.'

The Lake Poets were not, of course, the first to write about the Lake District, and frequently they wrote about almost anything but the place to which they had been transplanted. As it has been estimated that some 50,000 books have been written concerning the Lakes, they were also clearly far from the last to write about it, and should be seen as an element in an ongoing literary tradition, albeit a very important element.

The Lake Poets were part of the 'Romantic' movement in literature, a movement which embraced Blake, Burns, Byron, Keats and Shelley, and was characterised by an emphasis on the natural, imaginative and emotional. There was a reaction against the classical, reasoned, structured approach of the earlier eighteenth century – not only in literature, but in all the arts. The Romantics were writing at a time of political and social upheaval, with the American Declaration of Independence occurring in 1776, the French Revolution beginning in 1789, and France declaring war on England in 1793. Britain was in the throes of an industrial revolution, with a major shift of population from the countryside into towns and cities.

A spirit of revolution informed romantic writing, allowing a freedom to explore new poetic subjects, and to explore them in radical forms and styles. Wordsworth was at the forefront of the revolution, and nobody embraced the romantic tenets of the importance of personal experience and the relationship between human life and nature more fully. According to William Hazlitt, Wordsworth's work was '... a pure emanation of the Spirit of the Age.'

Acknowledgements

Sincere thanks are due to Chris McCully, Helen Maclean, Ruth Campbell, Nancy Martin, Alex Black, Michael Mitchell and Sally Woodhead for their practical criticism, advice and encouragement. Special thanks also to Ed Geldard, whose beautiful photographs help to bring the world of the Lake Poets to life.

William Wordsworth
(1770–1850)

The American poet Robert Frost wrote 'I was never a radical in my youth because I didn't want to be a Conservative when I got old,' and of all English poets, William Wordsworth is perhaps the most famous example of a radical youth who grew into an old Conservative.

Coleridge wrote in 1800 that Wordsworth was '... a greater poet than any since Milton,' and Keats considered him to be '... deeper than Milton,' declaring that he could '... think into the human heart.' The Poet Laureate Ted Hughes writes '... when you look back, Wordsworth is the first mountain-range you see.' More than any other English writer, Wordsworth was a poet of place, and the founder of the school of 'Lake Poets' was a Lake Poet in terms of subject matter as well as residential qualifications. Unlike other writers of the school, Wordsworth was a native Cumbrian, born on the outskirts of the Lake District.

As a young man, Wordsworth was not only a political radical, but also a poetic radical. He rejected the prevailing fondness for elaborate imagery and elevated subject matter, and chose

Crummock Water
Crummock Water entranced Wordsworth. He wrote, 'there is scarcely anything finer than the view from a boat in the centre of Crummock-water.'

instead to write in a simpler, more direct style, which he felt was close to the speech of the common man. He was passionately interested in the natural world, and he wrote about topics which had previously been considered unworthy of attention by poets. In chronicling the lives of those marginalised in society he expressed some of the ideals of equality and fraternity that characterised the French Revolution. In the preface to the second edition of *Lyrical Ballads*, Wordsworth stated that 'Poetry is the spontaneous overflow of powerful feelings: it takes its origin from emotion recollected in tranquillity ....' His intention, he wrote, was 'to make the incidents of common life interesting by tracing in them ... the primary laws of our nature.'

Not everyone was impressed by Wordsworth's notion of poetry, however, and Southey wrote in a review of the 1807 collection *Poems in Two Volumes* that Wordsworth was guilty of seeing '... pile-worts and daffodowndillies through the same telescope which he applies to the moon and stars.' He also accused him of finding '... subjects for philosophising and fine feeling in every peasant and vagabond.' That notable opponent of the 'Lakes School' Lord Byron was less subtle, dismissing the poems as '... namby-pamby trash ....'

Such criticism must have stung Wordsworth, but he never lacked confidence in his own ability as a writer. Norman Nicholson described Wordsworth as '... one of the supreme examples of the egoist in poetry,' noting that 'he knew that he had to drive all his faculties, all his powers of experience, for the one purpose. The poetry justified the egoism.' Local people around Grasmere and Rydal found Wordsworth aloof, despite the fact that of all poets he purported to be interested in the 'common man'. His habit of composing poetry while walking out of doors probably added to his reputation for unapproachability. Hartley Coleridge was reputedly told by a stone-breaker he met while walking one day, '... auld Wadsworth frae Rydal's brokken lowce ageean, and gaes booing his pottery up an' doon roads, sometimes never seein' a body at aw', an' anudder time talking as sensible as owder you or me!'

William Hazlitt, writing in 1818, described Wordsworth as '... in his person above the middle size, with marked features, and an air somewhat stately and Quixotic ... He has a peculiar sweetness in his smile, and great depth and manliness and a rugged harmony, in the tone of his voice. His manner of reading his own poetry is particularly imposing; and in his favourite passages his eye beams with preternatural lustre, and the meaning labours slowly up from his swelling breast ... It is clear that he is either mad or inspired ... His standard of poetry is high and severe, almost to exclusiveness. He admits of nothing below, scarcely of anything above himself.'

William Wordsworth was born in Cockermouth, Cumberland, on 7 April 1770, the second child in what was to be a family of four boys and a girl.

Kirkstile Village
The village of Kirkstile is only a short distance from Cockermouth, the birthplace of
Wordsworth.

Wordsworth's birthplace on the Main Street belonged to Sir John Lowther,
for whom his father, John, worked as a land agent. After Wordsworth's
mother, Ann, died in 1778, he and his elder brother Richard were sent to the
grammar school at Hawkshead, lodging with Ann Tyson. William's time at
the grammar school was happy and productive, and here he first began to
write poetry. His father died when William was thirteen years old, and the
loss of a father while still young was an experience Wordsworth shared with
Coleridge and de Quincey. In October 1787, Wordsworth left what he called

17

his 'native regions' for the first time in order to enter St John's College, Cambridge University.

His university career was solid but undistinguished, and in the summer of 1790 he made his first tour of France and Switzerland in the company of a fellow undergraduate, Robert Jones. He returned to France late in 1791, on a visit that was to prove more significant.

Wordsworth became a convert to republicanism, and embraced the French revolution, also falling in love with Annette Vallon in Orleans. She bore him an illegitimate daughter, Caroline, in December 1792, a fact that only came to light during the twentieth century. It seems likely that the couple intended to marry, but the royalist Vallon family was hostile to Wordsworth, and the situation was further complicated by France's declaration of war on England. Wordsworth returned home before the birth of his daughter. In 1793, his first poems – *An Evening Walk* and *Descriptive Sketches* – were published.

In January 1795, Wordsworth inherited £900 from Raisley Calvert, brother of a school friend, and this gave him the freedom to dedicate himself to writing poetry. In the autumn of that year, William and sister Dorothy set up home in the West Country, initially at Racedown in Dorset, and then at Alfoxden in Somerset, close to where Coleridge was living at Nether Stowey. The friendship between Wordsworth and Coleridge flourished in one of the most fruitful (although, in truth, relatively short-lived) literary collaborations of all time, and most of the poems that were to comprise *Lyrical Ballads* (published 1798) were written in 1797/98, including Wordsworth's *The Ruined Cottage*, *Tintern Abbey* and the 'Lucy Poems'.

Towards the end of 1799, Wordsworth and Coleridge undertook a walking tour of the Lake District, where Wordsworth discovered that Dove Cottage at Town End, Grasmere, was available to rent. The idea of returning to his native country to write strongly appealed, and by late December of that same year William and Dorothy were installed in Dove Cottage. The next eight and a half years were to prove some of the happiest for the Wordsworths, and some of the most productive in terms of William's poetic output. In 1805 he completed an early version of his great autobiographical work *The Prelude*, and two years later *Poems in Two Volumes* was published, containing most of the poetry written since the second edition of *Lyrical Ballads* in 1801. At the time, this book received mixed critical reviews, but it contained a number of what have become Wordsworth's best-known poems, including *I Wandered Lonely As a Cloud*, *Resolution and Independence*, *The Solitary Reaper*, *Composed upon Westminster Bridge*, *My Heart Leaps up* and the ode *Intimations of Immortality*.

In the summer of 1802, the Wordsworth finances received a boost when the Lowthers repaid a debt originally owed to William's father, and in October of that year William married Mary Hutchinson, a childhood friend of the family.

Path along Ullswater
Skirting the eastern edge of Ullswater is an old pony track once used by packhorse traders and smugglers with ponies laden with contraband.

Grasmere Village
Wordsworth is buried in the churchyard here.

1803 saw William and Dorothy touring Scotland, accompanied for a time by Coleridge, and the tour produced a number of poems and a meeting with Walter Scott. One particular sadness of the Dove Cottage years was the drowning in February 1805 of William and Dorothy's younger brother, John, Captain of the East India Company ship, *The Earl of Abergavenny*. While at Dove Cottage, Mary gave birth to three children, John, Thomas and Dora, and lack of space for the growing family necessitated a move to a larger house. In May 1808, with a fourth child expected, the Wordsworths became tenants of Allan Bank, a recently-built house close to Grasmere village. For two years from May 1811, the family lived in Grasmere Rectory, but this was not a happy time for them as three-year-old Catharine and six-year-old Thomas both died in 1812. The sight of their graves in the churchyard opposite the rectory was more than the Wordsworths could bear, and in May 1813 they moved to Rydal Mount, half way between Grasmere and Ambleside.

Church at Buttermere
Wordsworth wrote eloquently of Buttermere and was deeply inspired by the small church.

This was to be the last home of William, Dorothy and Mary, and biographers have found it convenient to contrast the young, radical, creatively brilliant Wordsworth of the Dove Cottage period with the old, reactionary, uncreative Wordsworth of the Rydal Mount years. This is an over-simplification, but it does contain some truth. The supporter of the French revolution became an opponent of the 1832 Reform Bill, an Anglican Tory who complained that the railways were '... transferring at once large bodies of uneducated persons' to the Lake District. In 1813, Wordsworth was appointed Distributor of Stamps for the county of Westmorland, a position which was effectively that of tax agent, and which brought with it a salary of £300 per year. In 1842, Sir Robert Peel awarded him a similar annual sum as a Civil List Pension, and his establishment credentials were underlined by his appointment as Poet Laureate on the death of Southey in 1843.

Windermere, Victorian Steamboats
In his *Guide to the Lakes*, published in 1810, Wordsworth suggested starting the tour at Windermere.

The lack of Coleridge's regular stimulus, and an increasingly respectable and comfortable lifestyle, did serve to blunt Wordsworth's poetic sensibilities, though in 1820 his volume of *Duddon Sonnets* appeared, complete with his prose *Guide Through the District of the Lakes*, which went on to appear in various guises during the rest of Wordsworth's life and up to the present day. So well-known did the *Guide* become that one clergyman who praised the book in Wordsworth's presence innocently asked if its author had written anything else. Little that Wordsworth wrote during the thirty-seven years he lived at Rydal Mount matched the early originality and intensity of work produced during the Great Decade that embraced *Lyrical Ballads* and *Poems in Two Volumes*, but he did keep writing, and there were flashes of greatness during the later years, including the *Duddon Sonnets, Surprised by Joy* – on the death of Catharine – and the beautiful 1835 *Extempore Effusion upon the Death of James Hogg*. A revision of *The Prelude* – finally published in fourteen volumes after Wordsworth's death – was also completed at Rydal Mount. Ironically, what is probably the greatest poem of the Romantic Age never appeared in Wordsworth's lifetime, and was published in the middle of the Victorian period.

At Rydal Mount, Wordsworth became a 'Grand Old Man' of English poetry, and many visitors, both invited and uninvited, made their way to the house,

Waterfall, Duddon Valley
Celebrated in a sonnet sequence by Wordsworth, the Duddon runs from the southern slopes of Pike O' Blisco to the sea.

though not all of them got past the gates. In 1849, the twelve-year-old Algernon Charles Swinburne was brought by his parents to meet Wordsworth. The Laureate read him Gray's *Elegy* and said as the Swinburnes left, 'I do not think, Algernon, that you will forget me.' At this point the young poet-to-be burst into tears.

The last years of Wordsworth's life were tinged with sadness at Dorothy's mental decline, and the death of his daughter Dora in 1847 was a severe blow. In the spring of 1850, Wordsworth caught a cold while walking and died of pleurisy on 23 April, the anniversary of Shakespeare's death and sixteen days after his eightieth birthday. He was buried in Grasmere churchyard, where he was joined five years later by Dorothy, and after a further four years by Mary.

Wordsworth's Grave , Grasmere
St Oswald's churchyard, Grasmere. The yew trees in the churchyard were planted by Wordsworth himself.

The Selection

Strange Fits of Passion Have I Known (1799)

Like the subsequent poem, *She Dwelt ...*, *Strange Fits of Passion Have I Known* was written in 1799 and published in *Lyrical Ballads* the following year. These are two of the '*Lucy* Poems', and were written in Goslar, Germany, though earlier drafts from the previous year exist in a letter of December 1798, from William and Dorothy to Coleridge. There is nothing to suggest that Lucy was a real person, and the poems probably reflect Wordsworth's affection for his sister.

Strange fits of passion have I known:
And I will dare to tell,
But in the Lover's ear alone,
What once to me befell.

When she I loved looked every day
Fresh as a rose in June,
I to her cottage bent my way,
Beneath an evening-moon.

Upon the moon I fixed my eye,
All over the wide lea;
With quickening pace my horse drew nigh
Those paths so dear to me.

And now we reached the orchard-plot;
And, as we climbed the hill,
The sinking moon to Lucy's cot
Came near, and nearer still.

In one of those sweet dreams I slept,
Kind Nature's gentlest boon!
And all the while my eyes I kept
On the descending moon.

My horse moved on; hoof after hoof
He raised, and never stopped:
When down behind the cottage roof,
At once, the bright moon dropped.

What fond and wayward thoughts will slide
  Into a Lover's head!
'O mercy!' to myself I cried,
'If Lucy should be dead!'

She Dwelt Among Th'untrodden Ways (1799)

She dwelt among the untrodden ways
    Beside the springs of Dove,
A Maid whom there were none to praise
    And very few to love:
A violet by a mossy stone
    Half hidden from the eye!
– Fair as a star, when only one
    Is shining in the sky.

She lived unknown, and few could know
    When Lucy ceased to be;
But she is in her grave, and, oh,
    The difference to me!

Michael (1800)

The following is an extract from *Michael*, which was
written at Dove Cottage in 1800 for the second
edition of *Lyrical Ballads*. Wordsworth subtitles *Michael*
'A Pastoral Poem', but this is a pastoral poem far
removed from the classical conventions of the genre.
Wordsworth's shepherds have real names and speak in
something like everyday speech, and the style is spare
rather than ornate. The naturalness of the language
and the blank verse style give the poem a quiet power.

Helm Crag Summit Ridge
Known as the 'Lady at the Piano', the summit rocks of Helm
Crag were described by Wordsworth as a 'Dread pair that, spite
wind and weather,/Still sit upon Helm Crag together.'

Upon the forest-side in Grasmere Vale
There dwelt a Shepherd, Michael was his name;
An old man, stout of heart, and strong of limb.
His bodily frame had been from youth to age
Of an unusual strength: his mind was keen,
Intense and frugal, apt for all affairs,
And in his shepherd's calling he was prompt
And watchful more than ordinary men.
Hence had he learned the meaning of all winds,
Of blasts of every tone; and, oftentimes,
When others heeded not, He heard the South
Make subterraneous music, like the noise
Of bagpipers on distant Highland hills.
The Shepherd, at such warning of his flock
Bethought him, and he to himself would say,
'The winds are now devising work for me!'
And, truly, at all times, the storm, that drives
The traveller to a shelter, summoned him
Up to the mountains: he had been alone
Amid the heart of many thousand mists,
That came to him, and left him, on the heights.
So lived he till his eightieth year was past.
And grossly that man errs, who should suppose
That the green valleys, and the streams and rocks
Were things indifferent to the shepherd's thoughts.
Fields, where with cheerful spirits he had breathed
The common air; hills, which with vigorous step
He had so often climbed; which had impressed
So many incidents upon his mind
Of hardship, skill or courage, joy or fear;
Which, like a book, preserved the memory
Of the dumb animals, whom he had saved,
Had fed or sheltered, linking to such acts
The certainty of honourable gain;
Those fields, those hills — what could they less? had laid
Strong hold on his affections, were to him
A pleasurable feeling of blind love,
The pleasure which there is in life itself.

Wordsworth acknowledged the importance of Dorothy's role in his life and work in a number of poems. This extract is from *Home at Grasmere* (1800)

> Mine eyes did ne'er
> Rest on a lovely object, nor my mind
> Take pleasure in the midst of happy thoughts,
> But either she whom now I have, who now
> Divides with me this loved abode, was there
> Or not far off. Where'er my footsteps turned,
> Her voice was like a hidden bird that sang;
> The thought of her was like a flash of light
> Or an unseen companionship, a breath
> Or fragrance independent of the wind ...

My Heart Leaps Up When I Behold (1802)

This poem first appeared in *Poems in Two Volumes* (1807).

> My heart leaps up when I behold
>   A rainbow in the sky:
> So was it when my life bega'n;
> So is it now I am a man;
> So be it when I shall grow old,
>   Or let me die!
> The child is father of the Man;
> And I could wish my days to be
> Bound each to each by natural piety.

Composed Upon Westminster Bridge (3 September 1802)

Wordsworth was greatly influenced by his reading of Milton, and as a result experimented extensively with the sonnet form. One of Wordsworth's most celebrated sonnets is *Westminster Bridge*, which may have been shaped by Dorothy's journal notes of the scene depicted in the poem (*see* Dorothy Wordsworth Selection). It was first published in *Poems in Two Volumes*. Wordsworth prefaces the poem with the observation that it was 'Written on the roof of a coach, on my way to France.'

Earth has not anything to show more fair:
Dull would he be of soul who could pass by
A sight so touching in its majesty:
This City now doth, like a garment, wear
The beauty of the morning; silent, bare,
Ships, towers, domes, theatres and temples lie
Open unto the fields, and to the sky;
All bright and glittering in the smokeless air.
Never did sun more beautifully steep
In his first splendour, valley, rock, or hill;
Ne'er saw I, never felt, a calm so deep!
The river glideth at his own sweet will:
Dear God! the very houses seem asleep;
And all that mighty heart is lying still!

I Wandered Lonely As A Cloud (1804 and 1815)

Unquestionably Wordsworth's best-loved poem, and the clearest example of
the way in which Dorothy's journal directly influenced her brother's poetry
(see Dorothy Wordsworth Selection). It was published in Poems in Two Volumes,
but revised in 1815 when a second stanza was added and other changes were
made.

I wandered lonely as a cloud
That floats on high o'er vales and hills,
When all at once I saw a crowd,
A host of golden daffodils
Along the lake, beneath the trees,
Ten thousand dancing in the breeze.

The waves beside them danced, but they
Outdid the sparkling waves with glee;
A poet could not but be gay
In such a laughing company.
I gazed and gazed, but little thought
What wealth the show to me had brought:

For oft when on my couch I lie,
In vacant or in pensive mood,

They flash upon that inward eye
Which is the bliss of solitude,
And then my heart with pleasure fills
And dances with the daffodils.

***

I wandered lonely as a cloud
That floats on high o'er vales and hills,
When all at once I saw a crowd,
A host of golden daffodils
Along the lake, beneath the trees,
Fluttering and dancing in the breeze.

Continuous as the stars that shine
And twinkle on the milky way,
They stretched in never-ending line
Along the margin of a bay:
Ten thousand saw I at a glance,
Tossing their heads in sprightly dance.

The waves beside them danced, but they
Outdid the sparkling waves in glee;
A poet could not but be gay
In such a jocund company.
I gazed and gazed, but little thought
What wealth the show to me had brought:

For oft when on my couch I lie,
In vacant or in pensive mood,
They flash upon that inward eye
Which is the bliss of solitude,
And then my heart with pleasure fills
And dances with the daffodils.

She Was A Phantom Of Delight (1804)

Mary Wordsworth was the subject of *She Was a Phantom ...* and William prefaces
the poem with the note 'Written at Town-end, Grasmere. The germ of this

poem was four lines composed as a part of the verses on the Highland Girl. Though beginning in this way, it was written from my heart, as is sufficiently obvious.'

She was a phantom of delight
 When first she gleamed upon my sight,
A lovely apparition, sent
To be a moment's ornament;
Her eyes as stars of twilight fair,
Like twilight's too her dusky hair,
But all things else about her drawn
From May-time and the cheerful dawn –
A dancing shape, an image gay,
To haunt, to startle, and waylay.

I saw her, upon nearer view,
A spirit – yet a woman too –
Her household-motions light and free,
And steps of virgin liberty;
A countenance in which did meet
Sweet records, promises as sweet;
A creature not too bright or good
For human nature's daily food,
For transient sorrows, simple wiles,
Praise, blame, love, kisses, tears, and smiles.

And now I see with eye serene
The very pulse of the machine:
A being breathing thoughtful breath,
A traveller betwixt life and death –
The reason firm, the temperate will,
Endurance, foresight, strength and skill –
A perfect woman, nobly planned,
To warn, to comfort, and command;
And yet a spirit still, and bright
With something of an angel light.

from *The Prelude* (1799–1805)

Wordsworth's greatest poem *The Prelude* was begun early in 1799 and completed in the summer of 1805, though he was to revise the poem throughout his life, with a final version being finished shortly before his death. It was originally intended as part of a much larger and uncompleted work, and the fourteen-book 1805 text is usually considered to be the 'standard'. *The Prelude* was published posthumously, and was subtitled ... or *Growth of a Poet's Mind; An Autobiographical Poem* at the suggestion of Mary Wordsworth. In *The Prelude*, Wordsworth traces his own development as a poet, and in the early books he looks back on his childhood, where the natural world influenced and stimulated his imagination.

from *Book First*

Oh, many a time have I, a five-years' child,
A naked boy in one delightful rill,
A little mill-race severed from his stream,
Made one long bathing of a summer's day,
Basked in the sun, and plunged, and basked again,
Alternate, all a summer's day, or coursed
Over the sandy fields, leaping through groves
Of yellow grunsel; or – when crag and hill,
The woods, and distant Skiddaw's lofty height,
Were bronzed with a deep radiance – stood alone
Beneath the sky, as if I had been born
On Indian plains, and from my mother's hut
Had run abroad in wantonness to sport,
A naked savage, in the thunder-shower.
Fair seed time had my soul, and I grew up
Fostered alike by beauty and by fear ...

from *Book Fifth*

There was a boy – ye knew him well, ye cliffs
And islands of Winander. Many a time
At evening, when the stars had just begun
To move along the edges of the hills,
Rising or setting, would he stand alone

Beneath the trees or by the glimmering lake,
And there, with fingers interwoven, both hands
Pressed closely palm to palm, and to his mouth
Uplifted, he as through an instrument
Blew mimic hootings to the silent owls
That they might answer him. And they would shout
Across the watery vale, and shout again,
Responsive to his call, with quivering peals
And long halloos, and screams, and echoes loud,
Redoubled and redoubled – concourse wild
Of mirth and jocund din.

                        And when it chanced
That pauses of deep silence mocked his skill,
Then sometimes in that silence, while he hung
Listening, a gentle shock of mild surprise
Has carried far into his heart the voice
Of mountain torrents; or the visible scene
Would enter unawares into his mind
With all its solemn imagery, its rocks,
Its woods, and that uncertain heaven, received
Into the bosom of the steady lake.

The World Is Too Much With Us (1806)

A sonnet included in *Poems in Two Volumes*, in which
Wordsworth laments man's increasing obsession
with the selfish and material, at the expense of
imagination and spiritual fulfilment.

The world is too much with us: late and soon,
Getting and spending, we lay waste our powers

Skiddaw from Keswick Fell
Wordsworth mentions Skiddaw in his poem *The Prelude*, 'The
woods, and distant Skiddaw's lofty height,/Were bronzed with a
deep radiance – stood alone'. Keats climbed Skiddaw in 1818 and
Robert Southey lived at Keswick from 1803 to 1843.

(Little we see in Nature that is ours),
We have given our hearts away, a sordid boon!
This sea that bares her bosom to the moon,
The winds that will be howling at all hours
And are up-gathered now like sleeping flowers
For this, for every thing, we are out of tune:
It moves us not. Great God, I'd rather be
A pagan suckled in a creed outworn
So might I, standing on this pleasant lea,
Have glimpses that would make me less forlorn
Have sight of Proteus coming from the sea,
Or hear old Triton blow his wreathed horn.

from *Ode: Intimations of Immortality* (1802–1804)

The eleven-stanza *Ode* was begun in 1802, and completed two years later, being published in 1807. The poem has the typically Wordsworthian theme of the loss of the visionary power of childhood.

There was a time when meadow, grove, and stream,
The earth and every common sight
        To me did seem
   Apparelled in celestial light
The glory and the freshness of a dream.
It is not now as it has been of yore;
    Turn wheresoe'er I may,
       By night or day,
The things which I have seen I now can see no more.

   The rainbow comes and goes,
   And lovely is the rose;
   The moon doth with delight
Look round her when the heavens are bare;
   Waters on a starry night
   Are beautiful and fair;
The sunshine is a glorious birth
 But yet I know, where'er I go,
That there hath passed away a glory from the earth.

A Complaint (1806)

Wordsworth prefaces this poem 'Written at Town-end, Grasmere. Suggested by a change in the manner of a friend.' The friend is Coleridge. *A Complaint* was published in 1807.

There is a change, and I am poor:
Your love hath been, nor lon'g ago,
A fountain at my fond heart's door,
Whose only business was to flow –
And flow it did, not taking heed
Of its own bounty, or my need.

What happy moments did I count!
Blessed was I then all bliss above!
Now, for this consecrated fount
Of murmuring, sparkling, living love,
What have I? (Shall I dare to tell?)
A comfortless, and hidden well.

A well of love – it may be deep
(I trust it is) and never dry –
What matter, if the waters sleep
In silence and obscurity?
Such change, and at the very door
Of my fond heart, hath made me poor.

Surprised by Joy (1815)

William's daughter Catharine died in 1812, aged three, and he notes, 'This was in fact suggested by my daughter Catharine long after her death.' *Surprised by Joy* is an example of one of the better poems written by Wordsworth after the 'Great Decade'.

Surprised by joy, impatient as the wind,
I wished to share the transport – oh, with whom
But thee, long-buried in the silent tomb,
That spot which no vicissitude can find?
Love, faithful love, recalled thee to my mind –

But how could I forget thee? Through what power
Even for the least division of an hour
Have I been so beguiled as to be blind
To my most grievous loss? That thought's return
Was the worst pang that sorrow ever bore –
Save one, one only, when I stood forlorn,
Knowing my heart's best treasure was no more,
That neither present time, nor years unborn,
Could to my sight that heavenly face restore.

from *The River Duddon: A Series of Sonnets* (1806–1820)

Like *Surprised by Joy*, the thirty-four-sonnet sequence *The River Duddon* is one of the best works of Wordsworth's later years. The Duddon is a river in south-west Cumbria. The sequence was written between 1806 and 1820, when it was first published.

XXXIV *After-Thought*

I thought of thee, my partner and my guide,
As being past away. Vain sympathies –
For backward, Duddon, as I cast my eyes,
I see what was, and is, and will abide.
Still glides the stream, and shall forever glide
(The form remains, the function never dies),
While we, the brave, the mighty, and the wise –
We men, who in our morn of youth defied
The elements – must vanish. Be it so!
Enough if something from our hands have power
To live, and act, and serve the future hour;
And if, as toward the silent tomb we go,
Through love, through hope, and faith's transcendent dower,
We feel that we are greater than we know.

Extempore Effusion Upon The Death Of James Hogg (1835)

A particularly fine 'late flowering' of Wordsworth's poetic talent, the *Extempore Effusion* was written within half an hour of his reading the death notice of

Wastwater and Great Gable
At first, Wordsworth disliked Wastwater, but later he was to change his mind about it.

his friend and fellow poet, often known as 'The Ettrick Shepherd'. In a long introduction to the poem, Wordsworth notes, 'The persons lamented in these verses were all either of my friends or acquaintance.'

When first, descending from the moorlands,
I saw the stream of Yarrow glide
Along a bare and open valley,
The Ettrick Shepherd was my guide;

When last along its banks I wandered,
Through groves that had begun to shed

THE LAKE POETS

Their golden leaves upon the pathways,
My steps the Border Minstrel led:

The mighty Minstrel breathes no longer
Mid mouldering ruins low he lies,
And death upon the braes of Yarrow
Has closed the shepherd poet's eyes.

Nor has the rolling year twice measured,
From sign to sign, its steadfast course,
Since every mortal power of Coleridge
Was frozen at its marvellous source —

The rapt one, of the godlike forehead,
The heaven-eyed creature sleeps in earth;
And Lamb, the frolic and the gentle,
Has vanished from his lonely hearth.

Like clouds that rake the mountain-summits,
Or waves that own no curbing hand,
How fast has brother followed brother
From sunshine to the sunless land!

Yet I, whose lids from infant slumbers
Were earlier raised, remain to hear
A timid voice that asks in whispers,
'Who next will drop and disappear?'
Our haughty life is crowned with darkness,
Like London with its own black wreath,
On which with thee, O Crabbe, forth looking,
I gazed from Hampstead's breezy heath.

As if but yesterday departed,
Thou too art gone before — yet why,
For ripe fruit, seasonably gathered,
Should frail survivors heave a sigh?

No more of old romantic sorrows
For slaughtered youth or love-lorn maid!
With sharper grief is

40

Yarrow smitten,
And Ettrick mourns with her poet dead.

Associated Places

As so many of the places associated with William Wordsworth had a common significance for Dorothy, brother and sister are treated together in this section.

William and Dorothy Wordsworth were born in what is now called Wordsworth House, a Georgian town house of 1745, situated at the west end of Cockermouth's Main Street. Their brothers, Richard, John, and Christopher, were also born there. The house has a walled garden which runs down to the River Derwent, and the sound of the river is an early childhood memory which Wordsworth records in *The Prelude*: '... the fairest of all rivers, loved to blend his murmurs with my nurse's song ....' Wordsworth House is in the care of the National Trust and regularly open to the public.

William attended Hawkshead Grammar School from 1779 to 1787, and his brothers were also educated there. The school was founded in 1585 by Archbishop Sandys of York, and contains the desk on which Wordsworth carved his name. Upstairs, the school library remains intact, and there is an account-book which belonged to Ann Tyson, with whom Wordsworth lodged, initially in Ann Tyson's Cottage in the centre of the village, and latterly in the hamlet of Colthouse, half a mile away. It was at Hawkshead Grammar School that Wordsworth wrote his first poems and was encouraged in his love of literature by the masters William Taylor and James Bowman. The school is privately owned, but is open to visitors on a seasonal basis.

Dove Cottage is situated in the hamlet of Town End, close to the A591 road to the south-east of Grasmere village. The property dates from the early seventeenth century, and was built as a hostelry, named the Dove and Olive Branch. It stood on what was then the main Ambleside to Keswick road. William and Dorothy Wordsworth lived there from 1799 until 1808, with Mary Hutchinson joining them after her marriage to William in 1802. Thomas de Quincey took over the lease in 1809, occupying the cottage intermittently until 1820, and continuing to use it as a book store until 1835. Dove Cottage was the place where Wordsworth wrote so much of his best work and Dorothy kept her journal, but it was also a literary home which was visited by a number of notable people.

Coleridge was a regular visitor, de Quincey first stayed in 1807, and Walter Scott and Humphry Davy both visited in 1805. Robert Southey and Charles and

Mary Lamb were also guests. The garden of Dove Cottage gave William and Dorothy particular pleasure, with Dorothy describing it as a '... little domestic slip of mountain'. It has been lovingly restored to a blend of the cultivated and wild, and is now much as it must have been in the Wordsworths' day. The Wordsworth Trust, which runs Dove Cottage, first opened it to the public in 1890, and a museum in a neighbouring converted barn enhances the experience of visiting the cottage with displays of important manuscripts and portraits, and with regular special exhibitions.

When Mary Wordsworth was expecting her fourth child in 1808, it became clear that Dove Cottage was simply not large enough for the growing family, and they moved to Allan Bank, just to the north-west of Grasmere village. This was the Wordsworths' home from 1808 until 1811, though in moving to Allan Bank Wordsworth was forced to swallow his pride as he opposed the construction of 'this temple of abomination' by a Liverpool merchant named John Crump in 1805. Wordsworth wrote to a friend at the time, '... this is a great vexation to us, as this House will stare you in the face from every part of the Vale, and entirely destroy its character of simplicity and seclusion.' De Quincey claimed that the house initially collapsed – much to the joy of villagers – while the builders were celebrating its completion in the Red Lion Hotel.

Coleridge stayed with the Wordsworths at Allan Bank during the winter of 1808–09, editing his periodical *The Friend* with the assistance of Sara Hutchinson, while de Quincey was also a guest, helping Wordsworth draft his pamphlet *The Convention of Cintra*, criticising British policy in the Peninsula War. The earliest part of Wordsworth's *Guide to the Lakes* was also written at Allan Bank.

In May 1811, the Wordsworths moved into the centre of the village to rent Grasmere Rectory, which dates from 1690 but was substantially altered and enlarged in the late nineteenth century. Two years later the family moved to Rydal Mount, following the deaths of Catharine and Thomas Wordsworth in childhood.

Rydal Mount was William's final home, and like all his others, it was rented rather than owned. This property was originally a farmhouse called Keens, which was enlarged in the eighteenth century and renamed. It belonged to the local landowning family of Le Fleming, who lived at nearby Rydal Hall. Much of Wordsworth's composition at Rydal Mount was done in the garden, and among the best pieces from the Rydal Mount years are the *Duddon Sonnets*, *Extempore Effusion Upon the Death of James Hogg*, and a final version of *The Prelude*.

Literary visitors included Hogg, John Wilson, Scott, Tennyson, and Keats, though Wordsworth was away canvassing for the Tory cause when Keats called. Having visited Rydal Mount, Tennyson declared, 'Never was a poet more comfortably housed.' Rydal Mount is open to visitors all year round.

Bluebells
Wordsworth was an avid gardener and landscaped the gardens at Rydal Mount with rhododendrums, daffodils, and bluebells.

Close to Rydal Mount is Dora's Field, accessible through St Mary's churchyard and now in the possession of the National Trust. Wordsworth bought this piece of land and threatened to build a house on it in 1826 when it seemed possible that he might be evicted from Rydal Mount to make way for his landlady's aunt. Later, he gave it to his daughter Dora, and today the field is renowned for its profusion of daffodils in spring.

The final resting place for many of the Wordsworth family, along with Hartley Coleridge, was St Oswald's churchyard in Grasmere village; it has become a place of pilgrimage for thousands of visitors every year. Along with William, Mary and Dorothy, William and Mary's children, Willie, Dora, Catharine and Thomas, are buried at St Oswald's, as is Sara Hutchinson, and there is a stone memorial to William's brother John. Inside the medieval church there is a monument to Wordsworth, with an epitaph by the Oxford theologian John Keble.

There are so many places in the Lake District associated with Wordsworth and which feature in his poetry; it is beyond the scope of this book to do justice to them. The definitive work on the subject is David McCracken's *Wordsworth and the Lake District: A Guide to the Poems and their Places*, published by Oxford University Press in 1984.

Dorothy Wordsworth
(1771–1855)

For more than a century after her death, Dorothy Wordsworth was viewed as little more than her brother William's close companion and amanuensis, but her role and her achievements have been reassessed in recent years, and Dorothy now stands secure as a literary figure in her own right. Dorothy made it clear, however, that she had no desire to be seen as 'an author', and her first concern in writing was always to record for others within a very localised group of family and friends, never with a view to general publication. This applies to her numerous travel journals, and in particular to her now celebrated *Grasmere Journal*, which was begun while William was away from Dove Cottage, so that, as she put it, 'I shall give Wm Pleasure by it when he comes home again' (14 May 1800).

The journal records everyday life at Dove Cottage in detail, and it provided Wordsworth with observations of places and events, which were frequently very useful to him when subsequently composing poems. Most notably, perhaps, this applies to Dorothy's description of the daffodils by the shores of Ullswater (*see* Selection). The journal has also proved invaluable as a reference source for generations of Wordsworth scholars. Dorothy has been called 'a poet in prose', and de Quincey captured the essence of her writing when he noted the way in which she could '... produce brilliant effects ... from something or other that struck her eye, in the clouds, or in colouring, or in accidents of light and shade, of form or combination of form.' Norman Nicholson wrote, '... her hands have the quick, living, nervous movements of an artist sketching from life.'

Like her brother William, Dorothy was an energetic walker, and together the pair spent much time out of doors. The relationship between brother and sister was spiritually intense, and Wordsworth attached great importance to Dorothy's journal-making. In *The Sparrow's Nest* he writes,

> She gave me eyes, she gave me ears,
> And humble cares and delicate fears,

Ullswater, Middle and Upper Reaches
The view from the upper slopes of St Sunday Crag commands Ullswater better than any other mountain.

A heart, the fountain of sweet tears;
    And love, and thought and joy.

The poem *Lucy Gray* owes its origins to a story initially told to Dorothy, and *Beggars, Resolution and Independence, Alice Fell* and a number of other poems all owe a debt to incidents and descriptions she first recorded. Some of her topographical writings were incorporated, in edited form, into Wordsworth's 1822 and revised 1825 edition of the *Guide to the Lakes*. Wordsworth's devotion to his sister emerges in *An Evening Walk, To My Sister, To A Butterfly*, and, perhaps most significantly, in *Tintern Abbey*, where she is recognised as the preserver and protector of the poet's memories. She is also acknowledged in *The Prelude* as a source of inspiration for William.

Dorothy Wordsworth was born in Cockermouth, Cumberland, in December 1771, one year and nine months after William, and she was the only daughter of five children. Following the death of her mother in 1778, Dorothy was sent to live with an aunt in Halifax, and when she was sixteen she moved back to

Cumberland to live with her grandparents in Penrith. Her time in Yorkshire had been happy, but her grandparents disapproved of her fondness for books and learning, and the Penrith years were comparatively joyless. From 1788 to 1794 she lived with her uncle, William Cookson, and his wife at Forncett Rectory in Norfolk. Her father had died in 1783, but Dorothy had not been allowed to attend his funeral, and had rarely seen her brothers since she was six years old.

In 1795, however, a legacy enabled William and Dorothy to set up home together; firstly at Racedown in Dorset, and then at Alfoxden in Somerset, where they could be close to Coleridge, who called Dorothy Wordsworth '... exquisite sister'. She was '... a woman indeed! – in mind, I mean, & heart – for her person is such, that if you expected to see a pretty woman, you would think her ordinary – if you expected to find an ordinary woman, you would think her pretty!... Her information various – her eye watchful in minutest observation of nature – and her taste a perfect electrometer.'

Wild Primroses
Wordsworth, writing in his poem *To the Small Celandine* has this to say on seeing a small yellow flower, 'Little flower I'll make a stir, like a sage astonomer.'

Between January and May 1798, Dorothy recorded aspects of daily life in her *Alfoxden Journal*, which gave her the model for her later Grasmere writings. In December 1799, William and Dorothy moved back to their native land to take on the tenancy of Dove Cottage, and from then until William's death in 1850 they were rarely apart. Dorothy's role in the Wordsworth household – both before and after William's marriage to Mary Hutchinson in 1802 – consisted of caring for children, domestic duties, gardening, and acting as proof-reader and copyist to William and sometimes also to Coleridge. When someone needed nursing, Dorothy was usually on hand, and she proved practical at arranging funerals and dealing with financial matters.

The *Grasmere Journal* was begun in May 1800, and continued until January 1803, just a few weeks after William's marriage to Mary. The wedding clearly affected Dorothy deeply, and she records in her journal wearing the wedding ring the night before the ceremony, which she was not well enough to attend. 'I saw the two men running up the walk, coming to tell us it was over,' she records tensely. Nevertheless, on a practical level, the enlarged Wordsworth household continued to function much as before, with Dorothy playing a vital domestic role, and getting on well with her sister-in-law, who was, in any case, an old school friend. The days of exclusive intimacy between William and Dorothy had, however, gone.

In 1803, Dorothy toured Scotland with William and for a time with Coleridge, and subsequently wrote a lengthy and detailed account of the expedition, astonishingly recalling all the details from memory, having taken no notes at the time. This journal, along with a second Scottish tour journal (1822) and a *Tour of the Continent* (1820), remained unpublished in Dorothy's lifetime. True to her self-effacing nature, Dorothy wrote her *Narrative Concerning George and Sarah Green of the Parish of Grasmere* (1808) in order to solicit support for the Greens' orphaned children, rather than with any intention of achieving literary recognition for herself. 'I should detest the idea of setting myself up as an author,' she wrote to a friend.

Dorothy also penned more than thirty poems, five of which were published while she was alive. Three poems appeared in an appendix to William's 1815 collection, and Dorothy was credited simply as 'A Female Friend of the Author'. Another poem appeared in an 1836 collection with the same credit, but when a final poem, *The Floating Island at Hawkshead*, was published in 1842, it was attributed to 'D.W'.

In 1829, Dorothy developed what would probably now be considered pre-senile dementia, an affliction described by the locals as 'faculty-crazed'. She wrote letters and poems which often have great poignancy during her increasingly brief periods of remission. In her last surviving letter from March

Langdale Valley
It was here, below Stickle Tarn, that the bodies of George and Sarah Green were found in March 1808. Dorothy Wordsworth wrote a narrative of the event and William wrote a poem called *George and Sarah Green*. The poem was not published until September 1839.

1838, she wrote to her niece Dora, 'My own thoughts are a wilderness – not pierceable by any star ....' Sara Hutchinson was her constant companion at Rydal Mount until she died in 1835, when the rest of the Wordsworth family cared for Dorothy until her death in January 1855. For the five years following William's death, she was tended by her sister-in-law and old school friend Mary Wordsworth.

The Selection

The following extract is from a letter to Mrs John Marshall (September 1800), in which Dorothy gives an insight into life during the Wordsworths' early days at Dove Cottage:

... We are daily more delighted with Grasmere, and its neighbourhood; our walks are perpetually varied, and we are more fond of the mountains as our acquaintance with them encreases. We have a boat upon the lake and a small orchard and a smaller garden which as it is the work of our own hands we regard with pride and partiality ... Our cottage is quite large enough for us though very small, and we have made it neat and comfortable within doors, and it looks very nice on the outside, for though the roses and honeysuckles which we have planted against it are only of this year's growth yet it is covered all over with green leaves and scarlet flowers, for we have trained scarlet beans upon threads, which are not only exceedingly beautiful, but very useful, as their produce is immense.

From Dorothy's first Grasmere Journal entry:

Wm & John set off into Yorkshire after dinner at half past two o'clock – cold pork in their pockets. I left them at the turning of the Low-wood bay under the trees. My heart was so full that I could hardly speak to W when I gave him a farewell kiss. I sate a long time upon a stone at the margin of the lake, & after a flood of tears my heart was easier. The lake looked to me I knew not why dull and melancholy, the weltering on the shores seemed a heavy sound ... I resolved to write a journal of the time till W & J return, & I set about keeping my resolve because I will not quarrel with myself, & because I shall give Wm Pleasure by it when he comes home again ...

Grasmere Journal (14 May 1800)

A fine frosty morning – snow upon the ground – I made bread and pies ... Helm Crag rose very bold & craggy, a being by itself, & behind it was the large Ridge of mountain smooth as marble & snow white – all the mountains looked like solid stone on our left going from Grasmere i.e. White Moss & Nab Scar. The snow hid all the grass & all signs of vegetation & the Rocks showed themselves boldly everywhere & seemed more stony than Rock or stone. The Birches on the Crags beautiful, Red brown & glittering – the ashes glittering spears with their upright stems ... The moon shone upon the water below Silver-how, & above it hung, combining with Silver how on one side, a Bowl-shaped moon the curve downwards – the white fields, glittering roof of Thomas Ashburner's house, the dark yew tree, the white fields – gay and beautiful. Wm lay with his curtains open that he might see it."

Grasmere Journal (12 December 1801)

Above:

Helm Crag (Winter)
In her journal of 12 December 1801, Dorothy Wordsworth wrote, 'Helm Crag rose very bold and craggy, a being by itself, & behind it was the large Ridge of mountain smooth as marble & snow white ...'

Right:

Foxgloves
In her journal of 22 December 1801, Dorothy Wordsworth wrote, 'The snow looked as soft as a down cushion. A yong Foxglove, like a star, in the centre ...'

Gowbarrow Park, Ullswater
It was here, while walking along the western shore, that Dorothy and William saw the daffodils that inspired his poem.

On 15 April 1802, William and Dorothy visited Gowbarrow Park on the shores of Ullswater. Dorothy later recorded her impressions in the journal, and some two years later, William wrote what has become his most famous poem, drawing on Dorothy's notes in the process (*see also* Wordsworth Selection).

> ... I never saw daffodils so beautiful they grew among the mossy stones about & about them, some rested their heads upon these stones as on a pillow for weariness & the rest tossed & reeled & danced & seemed as if they verily laughed with the wind that blew upon them over the Lake, they looked so gay ever glancing ever changing ...
>
> *Grasmere Journal* (15 April 1802)

One of the joys of the *Grasmere Journal* is the way in which Dorothy juxtaposes the literary and the domestic. The 'ode' mentioned is one of Wordsworth's finest poems, *Intimations of Immortality*:

A divine morning – at Breakfast Wm wrote part of an ode – Mr Olliff sent the Dung & Wm went to work in the garden we sate all day in the Orchard.

Grasmere Journal (27 April 1802)

En route to visit Annette Vallon and daughter Caroline in France in the summer of 1802, Dorothy and William stayed in London. Dorothy described the morning of their departure in her journal, and William captured the moment in one of his best-known sonnets, *Upon Westminster Bridge*. It is not certain, however, whether the sonnet or the journal entry was written first.

It was a beautiful morning. The City, St Paul's, with the river & a multitude of little Boats, made a most beautiful sight as we crossed Westminster Bridge. The houses were not overhung by their cloud of smoke & they were spread out endlessly, yet the sun shone so brightly with such a pure light that there was even something like the purity of one of nature's own grand Spectacles.

Grasmere Journal (31 July 1802)

The following is Dorothy's journal entry concerning the marriage of William and Mary. It is interesting to note that the formality of the opening sentence soon gives way to a much more emotional response. In the journal, the lines from 'I gave him the wedding ring ...' to '... blessed me fervently,' have been heavily scored through in an attempt to prevent anyone from reading them.

On Monday 4th October 1802, my Brother William was married to Mary Hutchinson ... At a little after 8 o'clock I saw them go down the avenue towards the Church. William had parted from me upstairs. I gave him the wedding ring – with how deep a blessing! I took it from my forefinger where I had worn it the whole of the night before – he slipped it again on to my finger and blessed me fervently. When they were absent ... I kept myself as quiet as I could, till Sara came upstairs to me and said, 'They are coming.' This forced me from the bed where I lay and I moved I knew not how straight forward, faster than my strength could carry me till I met my beloved William and fell upon his bosom.

Grasmere Journal (4 October 1802)

To My Niece Dorothy, A Sleepless Baby (1805)

One of three poems published in Wordsworth's 1815 collection, where it was titled *The Cottager to her Infant*. The Dorothy to whom the poem is addressed is William's daughter, commonly known as Dora.

The days are cold; the nights are long
The north wind sings a doleful song
Then hush again upon my breast;
All merry things are now at rest
    Save thee my pretty love!

The kitten sleeps upon the hearth;
The crickets long have ceased their mirth
There's nothing stirring in the house
Save one wee hungry nibbling mouse
    Then why so busy thou?

Nay, start not at that sparkling light
'Tis but the moon that shines so bright
On the window-pane bedropp'd with rain
Then, little Darling, sleep again
    And wake when it is Day.

Floating Island At Hawkshead, An Incident In The Schemes Of Nature

This poem probably dates from the late 1820s, and was published in Wordsworth's 1842 collection. It was the fifth and final poem written by Dorothy to be published during her lifetime.

Harmonious Powers with Nature work
On sky, earth, river, lake, and sea:
Sunshine and storm, whirlwind and breeze
All in one duteous task agree.

Once did I see a slip of earth,
By throbbing waves long undermined,
Loosed from its hold; – how no one knew
But all might asee it float, obedient to the wind.

Might see it, from the verdant shore
Dissevered float upon the Lake,
Float, with its crest of trees adorned
On which the warbling birds their pastime take.

Tarn Hows
The beautiful Tarn Hows, near Coniston, is one of the most visited places in the Lakes.

Food, shelter, safety there they find
There berries ripen, flowerets bloom;
There insects live their lives – and die:
A peopled world it is; – in size a tiny room.
And thus through many seasons' space
This little Island may survive
But Nature, though we mark her not,
Will take away – may cease to give.

Perchance when you are wandering forth
Upon some vacant sunny day
Without an object, hope, or fear,
Thither your eyes may turn – the Isle is passed away.

Buried beneath the glittering Lake!
Its place no longer to be found,
Yet the lost fragments shall remain,
To fertilize some other ground.

Thoughts On My Sick Bed (1832)

A poignant poem written when Dorothy was in the early stages of the mental illness which was to strengthen its grip on her throughout the last twenty years of her life. The penultimate verse refers to Wordsworth's 1798 poem *Lines Composed a few miles above Tintern Abbey*.

And has the remnant of my life
Been pilfered of this sunny Spring?
And have its own prelusive sounds
Touched in my heart no echoing string?

Ah! say not so – the hidden life
Couchant within this feeble frame
Hath been enriched by kindred gifts,
That, undesired, unsought – for, came

With joyful heart in youthful days
When fresh each season in its Round
I welcomed the earliest celandine

Glittering upon the mossy ground;
With busy eyes I pierced the lane
In quest of known and unknown things,
– The primrose a lamp on its fortress rock,
The silent butterfly spreading its wings,
The violet betrayed by its noiseless breath,
The daffodil dancing in the breeze,
The carolling thrush, on his naked perch,
Towering above the budding trees.

Our cottage-hearth no longer home,
Companions of Nature were we,
The stirring, the Still, the Loquacious, the Mute –
To all we gave our sympathy.

Yet never in those careless days
When spring-time in rock, field, or bower
Was but a fountain of earthly hope
A promise of fruits & the splendid flower.

No! then I never felt a bliss
That might with that compare
Which, piercing to my couch of rest,
Came on the vernal air.

When loving Friends an offering brought,
The first flowers of the year,
Culled from the precincts of our home,
From nooks to Memory dear.

With some sad thoughts the work was done,
Unprompted and unbidden,
But joy it brought to my hidden life,
To consciousness no longer hidden
I felt a Power unfelt before,
Controlling weakness, languor, pain;
It bore me to the Terrace walk
I trod the Hills again; –

The Kirkstone
Wordsworth had this to say of the Kirkstone, ' This block – and yon, whose church-like frame,/
Gives to this savage pass its name'.

No prisoner in this lonely room,
I saw the green Banks of the Wye,
Recalling thy prophetic words,
Bard, Brother, Friend from infancy!

No need of motion, or of strength,
Or even the breathing air:
– I thought of Nature's loveliest scenes;
And with Memory I was there.

When Shall I Tread Your Garden Path? (1835)

When shall I tread your garden path?
Or climb your sheltering hill?

Cotton Grass
To be found throughout the Lake District.

When shall I wander, free as air,
And track the foaming rill?

A prisoner on my pillowed couch
Five years in feebleness I've lain,
Oh! shall I e'er with vigorous step
Travel the hills again?

Associated Places

(*See* Wordsworth)

Samuel Taylor Coleridge
(1772–1834)

Samuel Taylor Coleridge was born on 21 October 1772, the tenth and last child of John and Ann Coleridge. His father was the vicar and grammar school master of Ottery St Mary in Devon, and before his death – when Samuel was just eight years old – he instilled a love of literature, philosophy and religion in his son.

Following the death of his father, Coleridge was sent away to Christ's Hospital School in London. Among his fellow pupils there were the future essayist Charles Lamb and critic, journalist, and poet Leigh Hunt. Even at this early stage of his life, Coleridge showed a keen interest in literature and philosophy, and his remarkable powers of oratory were already attracting admirers among his contemporaries while still at school.

Coleridge went up to Cambridge in 1792, and studied at Jesus College. Here he published his first poems – in the *Morning Post* – during 1793, and became associated with radical philosophy and politics, enthusiastically embracing the cause of the French Revolution. Even at this early stage there were indications of some of the weaknesses that would characterise his later life. He began to drink heavily and fell in love with Mary Evans, the sister of a former schoolmate – a passion that was not returned.

Because of a series of unpaid bills and his unrequited love for Mary, Coleridge left Cambridge for London in 1793 to enlist in the 15th Light Dragoons, but it very soon became clear that he was a less than competent soldier, and he was bought out under an insanity clause by his family.

He returned to Cambridge in April 1794 and in June met Robert Southey, who was studying at Oxford at the time and whose poetry he admired. The pair became good friends. This was an influential meeting both in terms of Coleridge's literary aspirations and also his personal life. In Bristol, Southey introduced his new friend to the Fricker sisters: Edith, to whom Southey was engaged, and Sara. Coleridge left Cambridge in December 1794, without taking a degree, and went to Bristol, where he wrote a series of pamphlets and delivered a number of lectures. In October 1795, he married Sara Fricker, while Southey proceeded to marry Edith.

Coleridge and his new wife moved to a cottage at Clevedon in Somerset, where their first son, Hartley, was born. By the time of his marriage, Coleridge was already taking opium on a regular basis, and he was to grow increasingly dependent on the drug during the years ahead.

When the critic and essayist William Hazlitt first met Coleridge in 1798, he described him as having '... a strange wildness in his aspect ...,' and wrote that '... his mouth was gross, voluptuous, open, eloquent; his chin good-humoured and round; but his nose, the rudder of his face, the index of the will, was small, feeble, nothing – like what he had done ... Coleridge in his person was rather above the common size, inclining to the corpulent, or like Lord Hamlet, "Somewhat fat and pursy".'

There was clearly a contrast between the body and the mind of Hazlitt's subject, and Hazlitt undoubtedly admired Colerdige's philosophical intellect. 'His genius ...,' he wrote, 'had angelic wings and fed on manna. He talked on for ever; and you wished him to talk on for ever.'

Coleridge had first encountered William Wordsworth in Bristol during 1795, and Wordsworth wrote of this meeting, 'I saw but little of him. I wished indeed to have seen more – his talent appears to me very great.' Then in June 1797, whilst living at Nether Stowey, Coleridge walked the forty miles to Racedown in Dorset, where he met William and Dorothy Wordsworth. Such was the impact of this meeting that only a month later the Wordsworths moved to Alfoxden, just three miles from Nether Stowey, in order to be closer to Coleridge.

The friendship which developed between Wordsworth and Coleridge was to have a profound significance not only for Coleridge as a poet but for the history of Romanticism. It was certainly the most important creative relationship of his life, and one of the most productive in English literature. Out of the meeting at Racedown came the collaboration between Wordsworth and Coleridge on *Lyrical Ballads* (1798). Coleridge's most significant contribution to this work was *The Rime of The Ancient Mariner*, which was to become the most famous of all his poems.

Lyrical Ballads represented a very real break from eighteenth-century poetic tradition, and is usually taken as representing the start of Romanticism, as it demonstrated such significant Romantic ideas as an interest in psychology, principles of democracy, and the power of nature.

There is much scholarly debate about which of the poets gave and gained the most from their collaboration, with one school of thought maintaining that Coleridge's 'conversational' poems gave Wordsworth the inspiration for his greatest works such as *Tintern Abbey* and *The Prelude*.

One critic even ventures the observation that as the friendship between the pair waned, so there was a falling off in quality in Wordsworth's verse, and

'The Cottage of the Solitary'
'And one bare dwelling;/One abode no more'. Wordsworth, *Excursion* Book II.

that Wordsworth was a 'creation' of Coleridge, and like all his best works he left him unfinished. Coleridge's poems *Kubla Khan* and *Christabel* were both uncompleted.

The opposing view suggests that it was Wordsworth — already the author of *Salisbury Plain* and *The Ruined Cottage* by the summer of 1797 — who gave to Coleridge a new and unconventional poetic style, and that William and Dorothy instilled in him the ability to 'see' nature — such a central feature of Romanticism (*see* Introduction).

From mid-1797 to 1802, Coleridge enjoyed five particularly creative years as a poet: during the first of those years alone he produced such notable works as *This Lime-Tree Bower My Prison*, *The Rime of the Ancient Mariner*, the first part of *Christabel*, *Frost at Midnight*, *Fears in Solitude*, *The Nightingale* and *Kubla Khan*.

This period also saw Coleridge gain a measure of freedom in financial terms; as early in 1798 he was given an annuity of £150 for the rest of his life by the brothers Josiah and Tom Wedgwood, of the eponymous pottery firm.

It was also at this time that Coleridge made his first visit to the Lake District. In the autumn of 1799, Coleridge went on a walking tour with Wordsworth, and during this visit William discovered Dove Cottage in Grasmere, conceiving the idea of moving there with Dorothy.

The prospect of again being close to William and Dorothy attracted Coleridge, and his interest in moving north was reinforced by the fact that in the same year he had met and fallen in love with Sara Hutchinson, the sister of William's wife-to-be Mary, whilst staying with the Hutchinson family in County Durham. William and Dorothy moved into Dove Cottage in December 1799, and in July of the following year, the Coleridge family took the tenancy of Greta Hall in Keswick, some fourteen miles north of Grasmere.

The damp climate of the Lake District did little for Coleridge's health, and his opium habit became more marked, with laudanum — liquid opium — becoming a staple part of his life. The local product of Kendal Blackdrop — a notorious mixture of opium and spices — was also taken. 'My health is as the weather,' Coleridge remarked in a letter, also describing his body as '... a very crazy machine.' Nevertheless, he was ecstatic about the Lakes and about his new home. He wrote in a letter to his friend, the scientist Sir Humphry Davy, 'My Dear Fellow, I would that I could wrap up the view from my House in a pill of opium & send it to you.'

Coleridge tried to woo eminent friends to the Lakes, with the intention of forming an intellectual and artistic colony, and in 1802 Robert Southey and his family joined the Coleridges in Greta Hall. Other friends, such as Humphry Davy and the writer and political philosopher William Godwin, failed to succumb to Coleridge's advances. Robert and Edith Southey were to remain at

Ennerdale Water
Ennerdale, the most westerly of the lakes, was one of Coleridge's favourite places. It is the only lake without a road.

Greta Hall for the rest of their lives, but early in 1804 Coleridge effectively left his wife after several years of progressive estrangement, living in London for a few months before travelling to Malta. The ever-responsible Southey stepped in and took on the added burden of providing for Sara and her three children, Hartley, Derwent and Sara.

Malta provided Coleridge with a healthier climate than the Lakes, and conveniently distanced him from his marital difficulties. When he returned to England after two years, he lived in London and with a variety of friends before returning to the Lake District in August 1808.

Here he lived with the Wordsworths in their new home at Allan Bank in Grasmere until May 1810, producing twenty-seven issues of his periodical *The Friend*, with the help of Sara Hutchinson. By this time, William and his wife

65

Mary had three children, and with Dorothy and Sara Hutchinson also resident, it was perhaps inevitable that tensions developed during Coleridge's seventeen-month visit. The intellectual strains of Coleridge's editorship of *The Friend*, along with his increasingly troublesome addiction to opium, did little to ease the situation, and the locals must have looked upon the bohemian household with some bewilderment.

Coleridge's relationship with Sara Hutchinson was always a troubled one, and finally Sara left to live with a brother in Wales, whereupon Coleridge briefly returned to Keswick, before moving to London, where he was to live for the remainder of his life.

Wordsworth's warning to a mutual friend, Basil Montagu, that his potential lodger Coleridge would probably prove a difficult prospect produced a sad estrangement between the two poets, which effectively lasted for eighteen years. Though their relationship had recovered to a sufficient extent to enable them to tour the Rhine together in 1828, they never recaptured their earlier productive intimacy.

In London, Coleridge was taken on as a long-term house guest by his friend and physician Dr James Gillman, in whose household he lived from 1816 until his death from heart failure in July 1834. Gillman successfully controlled Coleridge's opium addiction, and during his later years Coleridge established himself as a significant philosophical

Rydal Water from Allan Bank
'Grasmere,' wrote Dorothy Wordsworth, 'looked so beautiful that my heart almost melted away'. She was writing of this view. It was at Allan Bank that the partnership between Wordsworth and Coleridge came to an end when Wordsworth is reputed to have called Coleridge 'a rotton drunkard' who had 'rotted his entrails out of intemperance.'

influence on the early Victorians, earning from Thomas Carlyle the sobriquet 'The Sage of Highgate'. As well as Carlyle, Coleridge entertained such literary luminaries as Rossetti, and his old school friend Charles Lamb dedicated his *Essays to Elia* to him, describing him as 'an archangel slightly damaged'. Even his wife and daughter Sara visited him from November 1822 to February of the following year.

Despite his personal problems, Coleridge possessed the most significant and wide-ranging intelligence of the Romantic period, a writer and thinker for whom poetry was just one form of expression, though one commentator has noted that 'Poetry was at the heart of a wider concern with language and the power of imagination and ideas.'

Coleridge was an outstanding critic, and one of the foremost philosophers of Romanticism. As well as maintaining an abiding interest in religion, he embraced the new dynamism of scientific advancement; whilst in Bristol during 1799 he volunteered to provide Humphry Davy with an account of his experiences under the influence of nitrous oxide, popularly known as 'laughing gas', with which Davy was experimenting at the Pneumatic Institute.

This wide-ranging intellect had its critics – William Hazlitt accused Coleridge of 'dallying with every subject by turns,' and declared that he had '... flirted with the Muses as with a set of mistresses' – but it also had many admirers. Coleridge was described as having one of the two '... great seminal minds of England' by the philosopher John Stuart Mill, who considered that his fellow philosopher Jeremy Bentham possessed the other.

Although he is chiefly remembered as a poet, Coleridge was also a prolific and very influential prose writer. His greatest prose work *Biographia Literaria* – a major volume of philosophy, criticism and biography – appeared in 1817, while his reputation was further enhanced by the publication in 1825 of *Aids to Reflection*, and two years later by *On The Constitution of Church and State*.

It was surely no coincidence that as a poet Coleridge had produced all his best work by the time he was thirty years old, and that his most creative five years began with his meeting with Wordsworth in 1797, and continued during the time that the two writers enjoyed a close relationship and inspired each other's work.

It may be argued that Coleridge was a 'Lake Poet' more by virtue of geography than because the area inspired and informed his verse in the profound and incontrovertible way that it did with Wordsworth. The latter-day 'Lake Poet' Norman Nicholson called him '... a poet rather than a Laker,' unlike Southey, whom he describes as '... a Laker rather than a poet.'

Coleridge may be said to have made a contribution to the literature of the Lakes via the Wordsworths, and in particular Dorothy, whose *Journal* frequently reflects the influence of Coleridge's vision. In the case of her brother, Coleridge's influence is more by way of general encouragement and stimulation, but is nonetheless significant.

It is, however, in his notebooks and letters that Coleridge made his most important contribution to Lake District literature, and both include original descriptions of the natural scene. The notebooks written whilst Coleridge was indulging in serious fell-walking have been described as '... unrivalled as prose writings about the Lake District.'

Coleridge's biographer Richard Holmes writes that '... these prose-notations were a new form of Romantic nature-writing, as powerful in their way as his poetry; rapid, spontaneous, miraculously responsive to the changing panorama of hills he moves through, and containing a sort of telegraphic score of his emotional reactions.'

In terms of his poetic output during his time in the Lake District, Coleridge produced the second part of *Christabel*, the 'Asra' poems for Sara Hutchinson, and his last major poem *Dejection: An Ode*, as well as a number of less well-known pieces.

Wordsworth and Coleridge had very different temperaments and approached the task of writing about the Lake District in ways that were clearly quite diverse. It has been noted that '... each poet had a totally different way of *seeing*. Wordsworth had the eye of a camera, Coleridge the eye of a painter ... Wordsworth, scanning a fellside, noted with exactitude every boulder, every crag, every pasture in the dale, each bird in the sky. Coleridge saw "The Hill like a Dolphin so beautiful in the lines of snow ..."'

The two writers may have had their differences, and certainly they grew apart, but when Coleridge died on 25 July 1834, Wordsworth was able to say, simply and sincerely, that he was 'the most wonderful man I have ever known.'

The Selection

The Rime of the Ancient Mariner (1797–1816)

This is the most famous of all Coleridge's poems, and was written at Wordsworth's suggestion for inclusion in the collaborative *Lyrical Ballads* of 1798, to which it was Coleridge's major contribution.

The version usually read today was published in 1816, and differs from the original, which lacks the marginal prose elements and used more archaic vocabulary.

Wordsworth famously wrote of the *Ancient Mariner* in his preface to the second edition of *Lyrical Ballads*, '... the poem of my friend has indeed many defects,'

and it met with something approaching derision in some quarters when first published, even being the subject of a hostile review by Southey. Posterity, however, has judged it to be one of the great poems of Romantic literature.

Hazlitt wrote in 1825, '... it is unquestionably a work of genius – of wild, irregular, overwhelming imagination, and has that rich, varied movement in the verse, which gives a distant idea of the lofty or changeful tones of Mr Coleridge's voice.'

The poem is too long to quote in full here, but the first of the seven parts serves to give a flavour of the whole.

Part I

It is an ancient Mariner
And he stoppeth one of three.
'By thy long grey beard and glittering eye,
Now wherefore stopp'st thou me?

The bridegroom's doors are opened wide,
And I am next of kin;
The guests are met, the feast is set:
May'st hear the merry din.'

He holds him with his skinny hand,
'There was a ship,' quoth he.
'Hold off! unhand me, grey-beard loon!'
Eftsoons his hand dropt he.

He holds him with his glittering eye –
The Wedding-Guest stood still,

Haweswater
Haweswater is one of the most isolated and difficult lakes to reach. It lies in a wild and unspoilt landscape.

And listens like a three years' child:
The Mariner hath his will.

The Wedding-Guest sat on a stone:
He cannot choose but hear;
And thus spake on that ancient man,
The bright-eyed Mariner.

'The ship was cheered, the harbour cleared,
Merrily did we drop
Below the kirk, below the hill,
Below the lighthouse top.

The sun came up upon the left,
Out of the sea came he!
And he shone bright, and on the right
Went down into the sea.

And through the drifts the snowy clifts
Did send a dismal sheen:
Nor shapes of men nor beasts we ken –
The ice was all between.

The ice was here, the ice was there,
The ice was all around:
It cracked and growled, and roared and howled,
Like noises in a swound!

At length did cross an Albatross,
Thorough the fog it came;
As if it had been a Christian soul,
We hailed it in God's name.

It ate the food it ne'er had eat,
And round and round it flew.
The ice did split with a thunder-fit;
The helmsman steered us through!

And a good south wind sprung up behind;
The Albatross did follow,

And every day, for food or play,
Came to the mariner's hollo!

In mist or cloud, on mast or shroud,
It perched for vespers nine;
Whiles all the night, through fog-smoke white,
Glimmered the white Moon-shine.'

'God save thee, ancient Mariner!
From the fiends, that plague thee thus! –
Why look'st thou so?' – With my cross-bow
I shot the Albatross.

The Keepsake (1800)

One of the group of so called 'Asra' poems, written during 1800–02, which records Coleridge's love for Sara Hutchinson. Apart from *The Keepsake* – written at Greta Hall – these include *On Revisiting the Seashore, Ode to Tranquility, To Asra, A Day-Dream,* and *The Picture.*

The tedded hay, the first fruits of the soil,
The tedded hay and corn-sheaves in one field,
Show summer gone, ere come. The foxglove tall
Sheds its loose purple bells, or in the gust,
Or when it bends beneath the up-springing lark,
Or mountain-finch alighting. And the rose
(In vain the darling of successful love)
Stands, like some boasted beauty of past years,
The thorns remaining, and the' flowers all gone.
Nor can I find, amid my lonely walk
By rivulet, or spring, or wet roadside,
That blue and bright-eyed floweret of the brook,
Hope's gentle gem, the sweet Forget-me-not!
So will not fade the flowers which Emmeline
With delicate fingers on the snow-white silk
Has worked (the flowers which most she knew I loved),
And, more beloved than they, her auburn hair.

In the cool morning twilight, early waked
By her full bosom's joyous restlessness,
Softly she rose, and lightly stole along,
    Down the slope coppice to the woodbine bower,
Whose rich flowers, swinging in the morning breeze,
Over their dim fast-moving shadows hung,
Making a quiet image of disquiet
In the smooth, scarcely moving river-pool.
There, in that bower where first she owned her love,
And let me kiss my own warm tear of joy
From off her glowing cheek, she sate and stretched
The silk upon the frame, and worked her name
Between the Moss-Rose and Forget-me-not —

Her own dear name, with her own auburn hair!
That forced to wander till sweet spring return,
I yet might ne'er forget her smile, her look,
Her voice, (that even in her mirthful mood
Has made me wish to steal away and weep,)
Nor yet the entrancement of that maiden kiss
With which she promised, that when spring returned,
She would resign half of that dear name,
And own thenceforth no other name but mine!

A Thought Suggested By A View Of Saddleback In Cumberland (1800)

Although probably written in the autumn of 1800, this poem was first published
in the *Amulet* in 1833. It is one of a number of pieces based on Coleridge's early
experiences of fell-walking in the Lake District.

On stern Blencathra's perilous height
    The winds are tyrannous and strong;
And flashing forth unsteady light
From stern Blencathra's skiey height,
    As loud the torrents throng!
Beneath the moon, in gentle weather,
They bind the earth and sky together.
But oh! the sky and all its forms, how quiet!
The things that seek the earth, how full of noise and riot!

Blencathra and Tewitt Tarn
In 1800, Samuel Taylor Coleridge wrote *A Thought Suggested By A View*. It was published in 1833.
'On stern Blencathra's perilous height,/The winds are tyrannous and strong;/And flashing forth
unsteady light,/From stern Blencathra's skiey height,/As loud the torrents throng!'

To Asra (1801)

First published in 1893, *To Asra* was prefixed to the manuscript copy of *Christabel*,
which Coleridge gave to Sara Hutchinson in 1804.

> Are there two things, of all which men possess,
> That are so like each other and so near,
> As mutual Love seems like to Happiness?
> Dear Asra, woman beyond utterance dear!
> This Love which ever welling at my heart,
> Now in its living fount doth heave and fall,

Now overflowing pours thro' every part
Of all my frame, and fills and changes all,
Like vernal waters springing up through snow,
This Love that seeming great beyond the power
Of growth, yet seemeth ever more to grow,
Could I transmute the whole to one rich
Dower Of Happy Life, and give it all to Thee,
Thy lot, methinks, were Heaven, thy age, Eternity!

Christabel (Part II – 1801)

Coleridge's longest poem, *Christabel*, is an unfinished narrative, set in a medieval castle. The first part was written at Nether Stowey in 1797, and when he moved to Keswick in July 1800 Coleridge was confident of being able to finish the poem. Although Part II runs to some 350 lines, a narrative ending was never forthcoming, though Coleridge continued to imagine completing the work for the next thirty years.

Wordsworth rejected *Christabel* for the second edition of *Lyrical Ballads*, finally substituting his own poem, *Michael*; an act that did little for Coleridge's poetic self-esteem, though he loyally continued to do the lion's share of editing work on the volume.

Although Part I of *Christabel* is set in a legendary version of the Quantocks, the second part takes place against the backdrop of a Lakeland landscape, and the following extract is taken from the opening of Part II.

Each matin bell, the Baron saith,
Knells us back to a world of death.
These words Sir Leonine first said,
When he rose and found his lady dead:
These words Sir Leonine will say
Many a morn to his dying day!

And hence the custom and law began
That still at dawn the sacristan,
Who duly pulls the heavy bell,
Five and forty beads must tell
Between each stroke – a warning knell,
Which not a soul can choose but hear
From Bratha Head to Wyndermere.

Saith Bracy the bard, So let it knell!
And let the drowsy sacristan
Still count as slowly as he can!
There is no lack of such, I ween,
As well fill up the space between.
In Langdale Pike and Witch's Lair,
And Dungeon-ghyll so foully rent,
With ropes of rock and bells of air
Three sinful sextons' ghosts are pent,

Who all give back, one after t'other,
The death-note to their living brother;
And oft too, by the knell offended,
Just as their one! two! three! is ended,
The devil mocks the doleful tale
With a merry peal from Borodale.

from *Dejection: An Ode* (1802)

This is the finest poem written by Coleridge in the Lake District, and also his last great poem. It has been described as one of the most perfect examples of the Romantic ode.

It is usually thought to be based on a much longer verse letter to Sara Hutchinson, written early in 1802, and Coleridge specifically dates the ode as having been composed on 4 April of that year.

In this poem, Coleridge is influenced by his ill-advised love for Sara, his marital difficulties, his increasing physical ill-health, and his opium addiction. Above all, however, he is concerned with what he sees as the failure of his imaginative vision; his fear that the ability to write poetry has left him. Paradoxically, Coleridge created one of his most brilliantly imaginative poems out of the apparent loss of what he termed 'the shaping spirit of imagination.'

The Verse Letter to Sara Hutchinson, with its confessional details, was not published until 1937, though even in its original form it was really intended for a wider audience of the 'Wordsworth Circle' than just Sara. A version of *Dejection: An Ode* was published in the *Morning Post* on 4 October 1802, and the date of publication is significant as it was Coleridge's own wedding anniversary and the date of Wordsworth's marriage to Sara's sister Mary.

Towards Windermere from Blake Rigg
The vista from Blake Rigg over Little Langdale Tarn to Windermere.

Late, late yestreen I saw the new Moon,
With the old Moon in her arms;
And I fear, I fear, my Master dear!
We shall have a deadly storm.
Ballad of Sir Patrick Spence

I

Well! if the Bard was weather-wise, who made
   The grand old ballad of Sir Patrick Spence,

This night, so tranquil now, will not go hence
Unroused by winds, that ply a busier trade
Than those which mould yon cloud in lazy flakes,
Or the dull, sobbing draft, that moans and rakes
Upon the strings of this Aeolian lute,
   Which better far were mute.
 For lo! the New-moon winter-bright!
 And overspread with phantom light,
 (With swimming phantom light o'erspread
 But rimmed and circled by a silver thread)
I see the old Moon in her lap, foretelling
 The coming on of rain and squally blast.
And oh! that even now the gust were swelling,
 And the slant night-shower driving loud and fast!
Those sounds which oft have raised me, whilst they awed,
 And sent my soul abroad,
Might now perhaps their wonted impulse give,
Might startle this dull pain, and make it move and live!

II

 A grief without a pang, void, dark, and drear,
   A stifled, drowsy, unimpassioned grief,
   Which finds no natural outlet, no relief,
    In word, or sigh, or tear —
O Lady! in this wan and heartless mood,
To other thoughts by yonder throstle woo'd,
  All this long eve, so balmy and serene,
Have I been gazing on the western sky,
  And its peculiar tint of yellow green:
And still I gaze — and with how blank an eye!
And those thin clouds above, in flakes and bars,
That give away their motion to the stars;
Those stars that glide behind them or between,
Now sparkling, now bedimmed, but always seen:
Yon crescent Moon, as fixed as if it grew
In its own cloudless, starless lake of blue;
I see them all so excellently fair,
I see, not feel, how beautiful they are!

Broad Crag
In a letter to Sara Hutchinson, written in August 1802, Samuel Taylor Coleridge described the first descent of Broad Stand: 'O god, I exclaimed aloud – how calm, how blessed am I now – I know not how to proceed, how to return, but I am calm and fearless and confident ...'

III

My genial spirits fail;
And what can these avail
To lift the smothering weight from off my breast?
It were a vain endeavour,
Though I should gaze for ever
On that green light that lingers in the west:
I may not hope from outward forms to win
The passion and the life, whose fountains are within.

While the Wordsworths were travelling to Calais to visit Annette Vallon and William's daughter Caroline, Coleridge went on a walking tour of the mountains of the central Lake District in August 1802. He kept a journal of this tour, ostensibly with no greater purpose than to entertain the Wordsworths on their return, yet the journal contains some excellent descriptive writing. Perhaps the most notable piece describes Coleridge's unorthodox descent from Scafell by the rock face of Broad Stand. Norman Nicholson considered that '... in no other passage of Lake prose is physical sensation evoked so tangibly.'

It is interesting to consider that the writer of this piece was undergoing the sort of creative crisis of confidence that had so recently led him to write *Dejection: An Ode*.

> ... I began to suspect that I ought not to go on; but then unfortunately, though I could with ease drop down a smooth Rock of 7 feet high, I could not climb it, so go on I must; and on I went. The next 3 drops were not half a Foot, at least not a foot, more than my own height, but every Drop increased the Palsy of my Limbs. I shook all over, Heaven knows without the least influence of Fear ... My limbs were all in a tremble. I lay upon my Back to rest myself, and was beginning according to my Custom to laugh at myself for a Madman, when the sight of the Crags above me on each side, and the impetuous Clouds just over them, posting so luridly and so rapidly to northward, overawed me. I lay in a state of almost prophetic Trance and Delight and blessed God aloud for the powers of Reason and the Will, which remaining no Danger can overpower us. O God, I exclaimed aloud, how calm, how blessed am I now. I know not how to proceed, how to return, but I am calm and fearless and confident. If this Reality were a Dream, if I were asleep, what agonies had I suffered! what screams! When the Reason and the Will are away, what remain to us but Darkness and Dimness and a bewildering Shame, and Pain that is utterly Lord over us, or fantastic Pleasure that draws the Soul along swimming through the air in many shapes, even as a Flight of Starlings in a Wind.

A Beck In Winter (1804)

A fragment not published until 1912. The concluding lines are illegible in the manuscript.

Over the broad, the shallow, rapid stream,
The Alder, a vast hollow Trunk, and ribb'd –
All mossy green with mosses manifold,
And ferns still waving in the river-breeze
Sent out, like fingers, five projecting trunks –
The shortest twice 6 of a tall man's strides. –
One curving upward in its middle growth
Rose straight with grove of twigs – a pollard tree: –
The rest more backward, gradual in descent –
One in the brook and one befoamed its waters:
One ran along the bank in the elf-like head
And pomp of antlers –

THE LAKE POETS

A Sunset (1805)

First published in 1893, the poem – untitled by
Coleridge – was inscribed in one of the notebooks
written in Malta in 1804–06.

> Upon the mountain's edge with light touch resting,
> There a brief while the globe of splendour sits
> And seems a creature of the earth; but soon
>   More changeful than the Moon,
> To wane fantastic his great orb submits,
> Or cone or mow of fire: till sinking slowly
> Even to a star at length he lessens wholly
>
> Abrupt, as Spirits vanish, he is sunk!
> A soul-like breeze possesses all the wood.
>   The boughs, the sprays have stood
> As motionless as stands the ancient trunk!
> But every leaf through all the forest flutters,
> And deep the cavern of the fountain mutters.

Epitaph (1833)

This was Coleridge's last poem, first published the
following year, on the occasion of his death.

> Stop, Christian passer-by! – Stop, child of God,
> And read with gentle breast. Beneath this sod
> A poet lies, or that which once seem'd he.
> O, lift one thought in prayer for S. T. C.;
> That he who many a year with toil of breath
> Found death in life, may here find life in death!
> Mercy for praise – to be forgiven for fame
> He ask'd, and hoped, through Christ. Do thou the same!

Watendlath Tarn
Used by Hugh Walpole as a setting for *Judith Paris*, the second of
the four novels that form the *Herries Chronicles*.

Eastern Fells , Early Morning
Wordsworth and Coleridge were the earliest of fellwalkers and gained their inspiration from the magical light of early morning.

Associated Places

Greta Hall is located on a small hill at the northern end of Keswick, close to the River Greta, and in Coleridge's time it was owned by William Jackson, who carried out extensive work on the property shortly before the Coleridges moved in. The hall had originally been built as an astronomical observatory.

Jackson was a well-to-do carrier, and the model for the employer of Benjamin in Wordsworth's poem *The Waggoner*. He let the house furnished to the Coleridges for the not inconsiderable sum of £42 per year, and was persuaded to waive the first six months' rent.

Coleridge was captivated by the place, and wrote in a letter, 'My Glass, being opposite to the Window, I seldom shave without cutting myself. Some

Mountain or Peak is rising out of the Mist, or some slanting Column of misty sunlight is sailing across me; so that I offer up soap & blood daily, as an Eye-servant of the Goddess Nature.'

In April 1801, he wrote to Southey:

Our house stands on a low hill, the whole front of which is one field and an enormous garden, nine-tenths of which is a nursery garden. Behind the house is an orchard, and a small wood on a steep slope, at the foot of which flows the River Greta, which winds round and catches the evening lights in the front of the house. In front we have a giant's camp — an encamped army of tent-like mountains, which by an inverted arch gives a view of another vale. On our right the lovely vale and the wedge-shaped lake of Bassenthwaite; and on our left Derwentwater and Lodore in full view, and the fantastic mountains of Borrowdale. Behind us the massy Skiddaw, smooth, green, high, with two chasms and a tent-like ridge in the larger.

Coleridge is often described as the first of the fellwalkers, and to consider places in the Lake District associated with him is to consider mountain landscapes. He was an adventurous and sometimes reckless walker, who got to know the uplands intimately, and who defied his lack of sound physical health to a remarkable extent whilst walking. Richard Holmes argues that Alfred Wainwright is Coleridge's 'greatest inheritor' in respect of his writing about the fells.

It was not unknown for Coleridge to walk by the most direct route to visit the Wordsworths in Grasmere, firstly, and most famously, making the journey by moonlight on 29 August 1800, carrying the almost finished manuscript of Part II of *Christabel* in his pocket. He recorded the walk — by way of Great Dodd, Stybarrow Dodd, Raise, the 3,000 feet high Helvellyn, Dollywagon Pike and Grisedale Tarn — in his notebook.

Dorothy Wordsworth — whose *Grasmere Journal* details the frequency of Coleridge's visits to Dove Cottage — recorded that particular nocturnal arrival: 'At 11 o'clock Coleridge came when I was walking in the still clear moonshine. He came over Helvellyn. Wm was gone to bed and John also ... We sate and chatted till half-past three, W in his dressing gown. Coleridge read us part of *Christabel*. Talked much about the mountains etc etc.'

In return, the Wordsworths often visited Greta Hall, which subsequently became an annex of Keswick School. There are plans to develop it as a Coleridge and Southey museum and visitor centre.

Coleridge and the Wordsworths frequently met at a point close to the east shore of Thirlmere, roughly half way between Grasmere and Keswick, formerly marked by the 'Rock of Names', or as Coleridge and the Wordsworths usually termed it, 'Sara's Rock'.

Above:
Little Langdale, Early Morning
Wordsworth and Coleridge's long tramps across the Lake District are famous. Often they would set out as the sun came up to stimulate their minds for their writing.

Opposite, top:
Lingmoor Tarn
'The mountain tarns,' said Wordsworth, 'can only be recommended to the notice of the inquisitive traveller who has time to spare.'

Opposite, bottom:
Thirlmere
Thirlmere, south of Keswick, was created in 1879 by merging two smaller lakes to create a reservoir. Thirlmere has connections with William and Dorothy Wordsworth, Samuel Taylor Coleridge, and Mary and Sara Hutchinson.

86

Coleridge records in his notebook entry of 20 April 1802, 'Cut out my name & Dorothy's over the SH at Sara's Rock,' and Dorothy writes in her journal for 4 May 1802 that she and William parted from Coleridge at the rock, '... after having looked at the letters which C. carved in the morning. I kissed them all.'

The rock, with the initials of Coleridge, Sara Hutchinson, William, Dorothy and John Wordsworth cut into it, was blown up when the present (A591) road and dam were built in the 1880s. The Wordsworthian Canon Rawnsley collected fragments of the rockface with initials intact and had them built into a cairn positioned just to the east of the new road. In 1984, the pieces of rock were removed to Dove Cottage and re-assembled, and a bronze plaque now marks the site of the cairn beside the A591.

Robert Southey

(1774–1843)

Of all the writers connected with the Lakes in the first half of the nineteenth century, and perhaps even of all significant Romantic writers, posterity has dealt most harshly with Robert Southey. In his day he was one of the leading writers of prose and poetry, and undeniably one of the most industrious, but today his most enduring work is the children's classic *The Three Bears*. Together with Wordsworth and Coleridge he formed the trinity of 'Lake Poets', and lived in the Lake District for forty of his sixty-eight years.

Southey was born in Bristol on 12 August 1774, the son of a draper, and much of his childhood was spent in the home of an eccentric aunt, Miss Tyler, where he acquired his love of books and reading. He was sent to Westminster School, from which he was expelled for starting up an anti-flogging magazine, *The Flagellant*, and went on to Balliol College, Oxford, where his radical views were strengthened by friendship with Coleridge. While at Oxford he wrote the play *Wat Tyler*, and in collaboration with Coleridge, *The Fall of Robespierre*. In 1794, in common with a number of his literary contemporaries, Southey left Oxford without taking a degree.

His well-received and controversial epic poem *Joan of Arc* appeared in 1796, and during this period of his life he was also producing many of his most enduring short poems and ballads, including *The Holly Tree*, *The Inchcape Rock* and the anti-war piece *The Battle of Blenheim*. While living at Westbury, now a suburb of Bristol, in 1798/99, Southey penned more than fifty poems, many of them published in the *Morning Post*. 'I never before wrote so much poetry in the same space of time,' he was to note later. Though the quality of the output was markedly different, there are obvious parallels between Coleridge and Southey in that both had written the bulk of their best poetry before moving to the Lake District.

After leaving Oxford, Southey returned to Bristol, where in 1795 he secretly married Edith Fricker, sister of Coleridge's wife Sara. Edith was described by her niece as '... an exceedingly fine girl, but very inanimate.' In 1795 and 1796,

and again in 1800, Southey lived with his uncle in Portugal and spent time in Spain, becoming Britain's leading expert on the two countries as a result.

In September 1803, the Southey family moved to Greta Hall, Keswick, more for practical than literary reasons, as Southey was then no admirer of Wordsworth's work, though the two men did become closer in later years. They had first met in Bristol in September 1795, when Coleridge and the Fricker sisters were also present. For two years prior to the Southeys' move north, Coleridge had been trying to persuade his brother-in-law to join him at Keswick, and as Southey needed somewhere large – for his considerable library – and inexpensive in which to live, the attractions were obvious, despite Greta Hall's remote location in a damp climate. What finally brought the Southeys north, however, was the death of their baby daughter, Margaret, after which it seemed reasonable that Edith should be close to her sister in her grief. In all, Robert and Edith Southey had eight children, of whom only four survived beyond childhood.

Norman Nicholson's mischievous observation that Southey was '... a Laker rather than a poet' has already been noted, but the Lakes rarely figure in his writings, and Nicholson concludes that '... his only claim to the title (Lake Poet) was a residential qualification ... In the forty years that Southey was to spend in Cumberland, he became one of the most industrious, most conscientious, and one of the most admired writers of his day – but he never became a Cumbrian. He was respected, trusted, honoured, but he had few local friends.'

Buttermere Lake
Buttermere was the home of Mary Robinson, 'The Maid of Buttermere'.

Southey ventured out of doors only for necessary exercise, or in order to show off 'his' Lake District to visitors with almost proprietorial pride. He admitted that he liked rain and long, dark evenings, as they meant he was not distracted from his work. One could not imagine this statement being made by Wordsworth or Coleridge.

The contrast between Southey and his brother-in-law and next-door neighbour at Greta Hall could hardly have been more striking. Southey had a strong sense of duty and self-control, and routinely completed an awesome literary workload. He remains, however, a curiously unsympathetic figure. Nicholson wrote '... his solemnity, his pretentiousness, his very virtues seem cold and unamiable ... It is easier to pity Coleridge for (to all intents) deserting his wife than to admire Southey for protecting her. He lacks the very faults that would make him interesting.'

The first of Southey's long narrative poems – now largely dismissed by critics – was *Thalaba The Destroyer*, which appeared in 1801. It did not sell well. Coleridge wrote, '... the metre of *Thalaba* bears the same relation to metre truly understood that dumb bells do to music; both are I presume for exercise and pretty severe too, I think.'

Undeterred by such criticism and disappointing sales, Southey went on to write more Romantic epics featuring exotic myths, including *Madoc* (1805), *The Curse of Kehama* (1810), and *Roderick, The Last of The Goths* (1814), and despite the judgment of history, these poems helped to make Southey a major literary figure in his lifetime, though not everyone was impressed. One enthusiastic critic stated that '*Madoc* will be read ... when Homer and Virgil are forgotten,' to which Byron was quick to add, '... not till then.'

As a poet, Southey was a radical in that he experimented with almost every known form, turning away from the neo-classical preoccupations of his predecessors, and embracing the prevailing Romantic concept of writing about the rustic and humble, and those marginalised by polite society.

He was an indefatigable correspondent and journalist, most notably for the *Quarterly Review*, as well as an author, making a living by his pen not only for his own family, but also supporting Sara Coleridge and her children when Coleridge ceased to provide for them. As a prose writer, Southey has stood the test of time rather better than as a poet, and even literary enemies such as Byron and Hazlitt admired his prose style, with the former declaring his prose to be '... perfect,' while the latter wrote that his style could '... scarcely be too much praised. He is the best and most natural prose-writer of any poet of the day.'

Most enduring of Southey's books is his *Life of Nelson* (1813), which is in many ways a model biography, but in total he wrote some forty-five books,

Gough Memorial
Gough Memorial stands close
to the summit of Helvellyn.
Both Wordsworth and Scott
have written about the events
described on the memorial.

including *Letters From England by Don Manuel Espriella* (1807), which purports to be
a volume of correspondence from a young Spaniard on the subject of English
life. There is also the ambitious *History of the Peninsular War* (published 1823–32),
a three volume *History of Brazil*, lives of Wesley (1820), Cowper (1830s), and
Lives of the British Admirals (1833). His final literary achievement was *The Doctor, etc,*
which appeared in seven volumes between 1834 and 1847, having been started as
early as 1813.

In that year, Southey received the Laureateship, ironically just as he was
turning away from poetry to concentrate on prose writing, having received a
government pension five years previously. Southey was offered the Laureateship
only because Sir Walter Scott refused to accept it, but Scott was a keen admirer
of Southey's verse. Posterity, however, also remembers Scott more for his prose
– the *Waverley* novels – than for his epic poetry.

Southey completed a Wordsworthian metamorphosis from young revolutionary to establishment figure, penning his *A Vision of Judgement* in 1821. In this he took on what he clearly saw as the Laureate's role as defender of the monarchy, and in particular the reputation of the insane and recently deceased King George III. Byron, whose objection to Southey centred on his transformation from radical to reactionary, wrote a wicked parody – *The Vision of Judgement* – in response. Byron's *Don Juan* is ironically dedicated to Southey, and in the poem he writes, 'Thou shalt believe in Milton, Dryden, Pope;/Thou shalt not set up Wordsworth, Coleridge, Southey;/Because the first is crazed beyond all hope,/The second drunk, the third so quaint and mouthy.'

Southey's standing as a literary figure in his day can be judged by the fact that in 1835 he received a pension of £300 a year from Peel, but he declined the Prime Minister's offer of a baronetcy, largely on financial grounds. He also turned down a position with *The Times* newspaper in London which would have earned him around £2,000 per annum, and in 1826 he rejected the offer of a seat in Parliament for a constituency in Wiltshire. He had no wish to leave Keswick.

In 1837, his wife Edith died, and two years later he married the poet Caroline Bowles. His last years were marked by increasing mental decline, and a year after his second marriage he was unable to recognise Wordsworth. The sad image emerges of a man once passionately devoted to reading and writing books, finally unable to do more than take volumes from the shelves of his library and pat them fondly.

Derwentwater and Skiddaw
This beautiful spot enjoys many romantic associations; Shelley, Coleridge, Southey and Ruskin all spent their honeymoons in the area.

Crosthwaite Church, Keswick
Southey is buried here.

Southey died in May 1843, leaving 14,000 books in his beloved library. Wordsworth attended his funeral at Crosthwaite Church, Keswick, and subsequently wrote an inscription for his monument. He also succeeded Southey as Poet Laureate.

Judged alongside the finest poetic output of Wordsworth and Coleridge, even a very good poet might look lacklustre, and Southey was demonstrably not a very good poet. For the modern reader, one difficulty when approaching Southey is the sheer bulk of work – much of it at best indifferent. One of his faults was a tendency to opt for a simplistic morality in many of his poems, and he lacked imaginative subtlety. Perhaps his greatest weakness was an unwillingness to push himself emotionally in writing poetry. Nobody could imagine Southey attempting the equivalent of *Dejection: An Ode*. 'I have a dislike to all strong emotion,' he admitted – hardly a phrase one could have mistakenly attributed to Wordsworth or Coleridge. The latter observed 'The smiles, the emanations, the perpetual Sea-like Sound & Motion of Virtuousness, which is Love, is wanting –/He is a clear handsome piece of water in a Park, moved from without – or at best, a smooth stream with one current, & tideless, & of which you can only avail yourself to one purpose.'

The Selection

The Holly Tree

Written at Westbury-on-Trym, near Bristol, in 1798, and first published in the *Morning Post*, *The Holly Tree* is one of Southey's better, and most reproduced, pieces.

I

O Reader! hast thou ever stood to see
    The Holly Tree?
The eye that contemplates it well perceives
    Its glossy leaves
Order'd by an intelligence so wise,
As might confound the Atheist's sophistries.

2

Blow, a circling fence, its leaves are seen
    Wrinkled and keen;
No grazing cattle through their prickly round
    Can reach to wound;
But as they grow where nothing is to fear,
Smooth and unarm'd the pointless leaves appear.

3

I love to view these things with curious eyes,
    And moralize:
And in this wisdom of the Holly Tree
    Can emblems see
Wherewith perchance to make a pleasant rhyme,
One which may profit in the after time.

4

Thus, though abroad perchance I might appear
    Harsh and austere,
To those who on my leisure would intrude
    Reserved and rude,
Gentle at home amid my friends I'd be
Like the high leaves upon the Holly Tree.

5

And should my youth, as youth is apt I know,
    Some harshness show,
All vain asperities I day by day
    Would wear away,
Till the smooth temper of my age should be
Like the high leaves upon the Holly Tree.

6

And as when all the summer trees are seen
    So bright and green,
The Holly leaves a sober hue display
    Less bright than they,
But when the bare and wintry woods we see,
What then so cheerful as the Holly Tree?

7

So serious should my youth appear among
    The thoughtless throng,
So would I seem amid the young and gay
    More grave than they,
That in my age as cheerful I might be
As the green winter of the Holly Tree.

Sonnet: To Spring (1799)

This poem was one of the products of Southey's most prolific period of poetry-writing, and was composed in a former ale-house he rented at Westbury.

Thou lingerest, Spring! still wintry is the scene,
The fields their dead and sapless russet wear;
Scarce doth the glossy celandine appear
Starring the sunny bank, or early green
The elder yet its circling tufts put forth.
The sparrow tenants still the eaves-built nest
Where we should see our martin's snowy breast
Oft darting out. The blasts from the bleak north
And from the keener east still frequent blow.
Sweet Spring, thou lingerest; and it should be so,
Late let the fields and gardens blossom out!
Like man when most with smiles thy face is drest,
'Tis to deceive, and he who knows ye best,
When most ye promise, ever most must doubt.

Southey's most successful attempt at descriptive writing is *Letters From England* by the fictional Don Manuel Alvarez Espriella (1807); a work which deserves to be more widely read. The section devoted to the Lake District gives us valuable insights into an already commercially expanding community. Ambleside has '... the marks of the influx of money', and Southey's description of Grange in Borrowdale was described by Nicholson as '... in prose well-jointed, free-moving, and natural as a healthy body ....'

This village consists of not more than half a score of cottages, which stand on a little rising by the riverside, – built apparently without mortar, and that so long ago that the stones have the same weather-worn colour as those which lie upon the mountain side behind then. A few pines rise over them, the mountains appear to meet a little way on ... and where they meet their base is richly clothed with coppice wood and young trees. The river, like all the streams of this country, clear, shallow, and melodious, washes the stone bank on which the greater number of the pines grow, and forms the foreground with an old bridge of two arches, as rude in construction as the cottages. The parapet has fallen down, and the bridge is impassable for carts, which ford a little way above. The road from the bridge to the village is in ruins ...

from *The Poet's Pilgrimage to Waterloo: Proem* (1816)

A long poem, and one of the few of quality that Southey wrote while living in the Lake District, *The Poet's Pilgrimage* relates to the Laureate's visit to the battlefield of Waterloo in 1815. It is significant for the picture it gives us of the pleasure Southey took in his home at Greta Hall and in his family, as related in the Proem. The poem was published in book form by Longman, and opens:

I

Once more I see thee, Skiddaw! once again
    Behold thee in thy majesty serene,
Where like the bulwark of this favour'd plain,
    Alone thou standest, monarch of the scene ...
    Thou glorious mountain, on whose ample breast
    The sunbeams love to play, the vapours love to rest!

2

Once more, O Derwent, to thy aweful shores
    I come, insatiate of the accustom'd sight;
And listening as the eternal torrent roars,
    Drink in with eye and eat a fresh delight:
    For I have wander'd far by land and sea,
    In all my wanderings still remembering thee.

3

Twelve years (how large a part of man's brief day?)
    Nor idly, nor ingloriously spent,
Of evil and of good have held their way,
    Since first upon thy banks I pitch'd my tent.
    Hither I came in manhood's active prime,
    And here my head hath felt the touch of time.

4

Heaven hath with goodly increase blest me here,
    Where childless and opprest with grief I came;
With voice of fervent thankfulness sincere
    Let me the blessings which are mine proclaim:
    Here I possess, ... what more should I require?
    Books, children, leisure, ... all my heart's desire.

Stanzas (1818)

Along with the preceding poem, *Stanzas* was one of the best written by Southey at Greta Hall. Wordsworth reportedly said after Southey's death that it was '... a true and touching representation of Southey's character.' The dead of the poem are the subjects of titles in Southey's extensive library.

I

My days among the Dead are past;
    Around me I behold,
Where'er these casual eyes are cast,
    The mighty minds of old;
My never failing friends are they,
With whom I converse day by day.

2

With them I take delight in weal,
    And seek relief in woe;
And while I understand and feel
    How much to them I owe,
My cheeks have often been bedew'd
With tears of thoughtful gratitude.

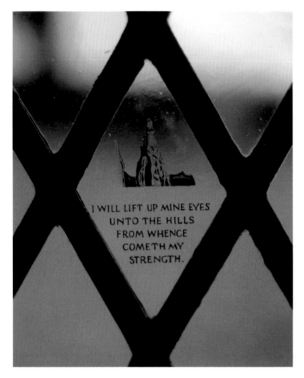

I WILL LIFT UP MINE EYES
UNTO THE HILLS
FROM WHENCE
COMETH MY
STRENGTH.

St Olaf's Church South Window
The memorial window to the members of the Fell & Rock Climbing Club who gave their lives in the First World War. St Olaf's is the parish church of Wasdale Head.

3

My thoughts are with the Dead, with them
    I live in long-past years,
Their virtues love, their faults condemn,
    Partake their hopes and fears,
And from their lessons seek and find
Instruction with an humble mind.

4

My hopes are with the Dead, anon
    My place with them will be,
And I with them shall travel on
    Through all Futurity;
Yet leaving here a name, I trust,
That will not perish in the dust.

The Cataract of Lodore (1820)

The most frequently anthologised of all Southey's poems, *The Cataract of Lodore* is a doggerel-poem, a clever exercise in rhyming, written by Southey for his children. The shape of the gradually widening poem imitates the waterfall, located just above the head of Derwentwater, as well as attempting to replicate its sound. The poem was first published in Joanna Baillie's *A Collection of Poems, chiefly Manuscript* in 1823. Here are the first and last stanzas:

'How does the Water
Come down at Lodore?'
My little boy ask'd me
Thus once on a time;
And moreover he task'd me
To tell him in rhyme.
Anon at the word,
There first came one daughter
And then came another,
To second and third
The request of their brother,
And to hear how the Water
Comes down at Lodore,
With its rush and its roar.
As many a time
They had seen it before.
So I told them in rhyme,
For of rhymes I had store;
And 'twas in my vocation
For their recreation
That I should sing;
Because I was Laureate
To them and the King.

Retreating and beating and meeting and sheeting,
Delaying and straying and playing and spraying,
Advancing and prancing and glancing and dancing,
Recoiling, turmoiling and toiling and boiling,
And gleaming and streaming and steaming and beaming,
And rushing and flushing and brushing and gushing,
And flapping and rapping and clapping and slapping.

Dungeon Ghyll Force

Wordsworth described this Langdale Valley waterfall in *The Idle Shepherd-boys*, 'Into a chasm a might block hath fallen, and made a bridge of rock:/The gulph is deep below;/And in a bason black and small,/Receives a lofty Waterfall'. Coleridge, too, was impressed and wrote that the colours of the waterfall ranged from white to blue.

And curling and whirling and purling and twirling,
And thumping and plumping and bumping and jumping,
And dashing and flashing and splashing and clashing;
And so never ending, but always descending,
Sounds and motions for ever and ever are blending,
All at once and all o'er, with a mighty uproar,
And this way the Water comes down at Lodore.

Associated Places

Greta Hall has already been described in relation to Coleridge, but it is worth stressing just what an important place it occupies in the roll call of English literary homes. Surely more letters, articles and books were written there than in any other house in the country. Most of Southey's epic poems, and all his major prose works were written in his beloved library, and distinguished literary visitors to Greta Hall included de Quincey, Charles and Mary Lamb (1802), Hazlitt (1803), Shelley (1811), and Scott (1813).

Southey's burial place of Crosthwaite Church is located half a mile to the west of Keswick town centre. Here the precocious eleven-year-old John Ruskin observed Southey attending a service in 1830, and wrote that his '... dark lightning-eye made him seem half-inspired.' St Kentigern's also contains the grave of Canon Hardwicke Drummond Rawnsley, one-time vicar of Crosthwaite, author, and co-founder of the National Trust, as well as those of Edith Southey and four of the Southey children. Southey's grave was restored in 1961 by the Brazilian government, in recognition of his promotion of that country and its culture. Inside the church is a splendid Gothic memorial to Southey, with an inscribed verse epitaph by Wordsworth. The new Laureate had difficulty finding exactly the words he wanted, and changed the ending of the inscription, as visitors may see from the alterations still evident in the chiselled lettering. The verse begins:

Ye vales and hills whose beauty hither drew
The poet's steps, and fixed him here, on you
His eyes have closed! And ye, loved books,
    no more
Shall Southey feed upon your precious lore ...

Thomas de Quincey
(1785–1859)

Were it not for the writings of Thomas de Quincey, our knowledge of The Lake Poets would be considerably impoverished, and in particular we would lack so many of the intimate, personal, and frequently amusing details that he was able to observe and record as a member of 'The Wordsworth Circle'. Where else but in the pages of de Quincey could one find the anecdote about Coleridge's father stuffing a lady's skirt into his breeches at a dinner-party, believing it to be his own shirt, or the description of Wordsworth tearing open the pages of an uncut book belonging to de Quincey with a buttery table-knife in his enthusiasm to examine it? At times it is as though de Quincey is having a conversation with an old friend. The essays are remarkable for their vividness and candidness. It has often been said that de Quincey was Wordsworth's best biographer. Although he was not a 'Lake Poet', de Quincey was unquestionably a major Lake Writer, and principal biographer of the Lake Poets and their families. De Quincey was an acute observer of the physical

Coniston Water
Wordsworth loved the view of Coniston Old Man from the lake. The lake is also associated with John Ruskin and Arthur Ransome's *Swallows and Amazons*.

attributes of those about whom he wrote, so it is fitting that Thomas Carlyle left a memorable description of de Quincey: 'One of the smallest man figures I ever saw,' he wrote, '... shaped like a pair of tongs; and hardly above 5 feet in all.'

Thomas de Quincey was born in Manchester in 1785, the fifth child of a comparatively well-to-do linen merchant. Like Coleridge and Wordsworth, he had to come to terms with the death of his father when he was still young, and Manchester Grammar School proved an unhappy experience from which he escaped in 1802, living rough in Wales for some months before moving to Soho, where he became friendly with a sixteen-year-old prostitute called Ann. When he lost touch with Ann and his funds were almost exhausted, he returned to his mother's home in the spring of 1803, and in May of that year he wrote what was to be a highly significant 'fan letter' to William Wordsworth at Dove Cottage, having been greatly affected by reading *Lyrical Ballads*.

Wordsworth – never immune to adoration – replied kindly, and issued a vague invitation to the young de Quincey to visit him in Grasmere. De Quincey got as far as Coniston on one occasion, and within sight of Grasmere on another, but was too shy to proceed to Dove Cottage and meet the man of whom he had become a devoted disciple. It was only in November of 1807, during the time he was studying at Oxford, that he met Wordsworth, and on this occasion he stayed at Dove Cottage for just a few days.

Once acquainted with the Wordsworths, however, de Quincey soon became very close to the family, staying at Allan Bank for several months during 1808/9, and then taking on the lease of Dove Cottage in 1809 and moving in twenty-nine chests of books. From 1820 he lived intermittently at Fox Ghyll, Under Loughrigg, using Dove Cottage as a store for his extensive collection of books. '... it happens that books are the only articles of property in which I am richer than my neighbours. Of these I have about five thousand collected gradually from my eighteenth year.' Sara Coleridge observed, 'Mr de Quincey's Books have literally turned their master and his whole family out of doors.' De Quincey had first got to know Coleridge in the West Country, and once Coleridge was living in the Lake District he borrowed extensively from de Quincey's collection, apparently having as many as five hundred books on loan at any one time.

The Wordsworths were less than delighted to see their beloved former home used as little more than a book repository, and never forgave de Quincey for demolishing their 'moss hut' in Dove Cottage garden, but their gradual estrangement from de Quincey had much more to do with his serious opium habit – a true addiction by 1813 – and his courtship of an eighteen-year-old local farmer's daughter Margaret – usually known as Peggy – Simpson, whom he married in 1817, three months after she bore him an illegitimate child.

Conveniently forgetting William's French indiscretion, the Wordsworths made no secret of their disapproval of the illegitimacy and de Quincey's subsequent marriage to someone of lower social standing. Dorothy Wordsworth wrote to a friend, 'Mr de Quincey is married; and I fear I may add he is ruined. By degrees he withdrew himself from all society except that of the Sympsons (*sic*) of the Nab ... At the uprouzing of the Bats and Owls he regularly went thither – and the consequence was that Peggy Sympson, the eldest Daughter of the house presented him with a son ten weeks ago ....' Margaret Simpson was a stabilising influence on de Quincey, and the marriage, which bore eight children, was a happy and successful one. Like Hartley Coleridge, de Quincey got to know the local dalesmen as real people, in a way that Wordsworth never did. Norman Nicholson made the telling observation that 'To the latter (Wordsworth) they were all definite articles: The Dalesman, The Statesman, The Solitary, The Pastor.'

It was only the evaporation of the remains of de Quincey's inheritance on books and a variety of extravagances – along with an ill-judged gift of several hundred pounds to Coleridge – that led him to become a writer at all. De Quincey's literary career did not really begin until he was thirty-five years old. Wordsworth's influence secured for de Quincey the position of editor of the local newspaper, *The Westmorland Gazette*, in 1818, but his insistence on including articles and news items concerning such inappropriate topics as German philosophy, Winchester Assizes and a South American incident involving a crocodile, meant that his tenure in this office lasted only until November 1821. It is remarkable that it should have lasted so long.

De Quincey moved to London, and his sensationally-titled *The Confessions of an English Opium-Eater* was published to great acclaim in the *London Magazine*, making him a literary sensation when it appeared in book form the following year. Despite the title, de Quincey was rarely an 'opium eater' as such, usually taking the drug as tincture of laudanum. The *Confessions* was de Quincey's equivalent to Wordsworth's *Prelude* and Coleridge's *Biographia Literaria*, in that it charts the development of the writer's mind from childhood to early maturity.

Back in Grasmere, de Quincey began to write for *Blackwood's Edinburgh Magazine*, and in 1830 he and his family moved to the Scottish capital on a permanent basis. The story of the next two decades of de Quincey's life is not happy, as he was forced on occasions to seek refuge in the debtors' sanctuary, at other times moving from lodging to lodging to evade his creditors. Unlike Wordsworth and Coleridge, de Quincey had never acquired a patron to cushion him against the fiscal unpleasantness of the outside world. In 1837, Margaret died, and he continued to live in Scotland until his own death at Lasswade in

1859, aged seventy-five. The last decade of his life saw some financial relief, as he received an income of £200 per year following the death of his mother in 1846. Whatever its ill effects, opium had effectively enabled de Quincey to write his greatest work, *Confessions*, and it can hardly be said to have shortened his life.

De Quincey was primarily a journalist, and his writings on the Lake Poets appeared in *Tait's Edinburgh Magazine* between 1834 and 1851. In their day, the articles were viewed by the people of Westmorland much as they might view tabloid newspaper 'invasions of privacy' today. It was not thought polite to intrude into the lives of respectable authors on the basis of personal acquaintance, and de Quincey does not shy from painting a 'warts and all' portrait of the Lake Poets, documenting his gradual estrangement from Wordsworth, whom he ultimately concluded was incapable of equal friendship, though he never faltered in his admiration for Wordsworth the poet. His Lake Poet essays were seen by many people as a betrayal of friendship and trust, and Coleridge's daughter Sara described the essay about her father as 'infamous.' The remark that Coleridge's '... marriage was not his own deliberate act, but was in a manner forced upon his sense of honour by the scrupulous Southey' outraged the latter. Southey urged the tiny and supremely unthreatening figure of Hartley Coleridge to 'Take a strong cudgel, proceed straight to Edinburgh, and give de Quincey, publicly on the streets there, a sound beating.'

Loughrigg Tarn
Wordsworth's description of this tarn, 'It has a margin of geen firm meadows, of rock and rocky woods, a few reeds here, a little company of waterlilies there', is still relevant today.

The essays have been variously collected, most recently in the Penguin Books volume *Recollections of The Lakes and The Lake Poets*.

The Selection

Wordsworth was, upon the whole, not a well-made man. His legs were pointedly condemned by all the female connoisseurs in legs that ever I heard lecture upon that topic; not that they were bad in any way which would force itself upon your notice – there was no absolute deformity about them; and undoubtedly they had been serviceable legs beyond the average standard of human requisition; for I calculate, upon good data, that with these identical legs Wordsworth must have traversed a distance of 175 to 180,000 English miles ... But, useful as they have proved themselves, the Wordsworthian legs were certainly not ornamental; and it was really a pity, as I agreed with a lady in thinking, that he had not another pair for evening dress parties ...

Meantime, his face – that was one which would have made amends for greater defects of figure; it was certainly the noblest for intellectual effects that, in actual life, I have seen, or at least have consciously been led to notice.

Wordsworth's face was, if not absolutely the indigenous face of the Lake District, at any rate a variety of that face, a modification of that original type. The head was well filled out; and there to begin with, was a great advantage over the head of Charles Lamb, which was absolutely truncated in the posterior region – sawn off, as it were, by no timid sawyer.

(Dorothy Wordsworth's) manner was warm and even ardent; her sensibility seemed constitutionally deep; and some subtle fire of impassioned intellect apparently burned within her, which, being alternately pushed forward into a conspicuous expression by the irrepressible instincts of her temperament, and then immediately checked, in obedience to the decorum of her age and sex ... gave to her' whole demeanour, and to her conversation, an air of embarrassment, and even of self-conflict, that was almost distressing to witness.

Nobody who knew him (Coleridge) ever thought of depending on any appointment he might make: spite of his uniformly honourable intentions, nobody attached any weight to his in re futura: those who asked him to dinner or any other party, as a matter of course, sent a carriage for him, and went personally or by proxy to fetch him; and as to letters, unless the address were in some female hand that commanded his affectionate esteem, he tossed them all into one general dead-letter bureau, and rarely, I believe, opened them at all.

Southey was, in person, somewhat taller than Wordsworth, being about five feet eleven in height, or a trifle more, whilst Wordsworth was about five feet ten; and, partly from having slender limbs, partly from being more symmetrically formed about the shoulders than Wordsworth, he struck one as a better and lighter figure, to the effect of which his dress contributed; for he wore pretty constantly a short jacket and pantaloons, and had much the air of a Tyrolese mountaineer.

Southey had particularly elegant habits (Wordsworth called them finical) in the use of books. Wordsworth, on the other hand, was so negligent and so self-indulgent in the same case, that, as Southey, laughing expressed it to me some years afterwards, when I was staying at Greta Hall on a visit – 'To introduce Wordsworth into one's library is like letting a bear into a tulip garden.'

Associated Places

Dove Cottage and Allan Bank (*see* William Wordsworth section).

In the early nineteenth century, the Simpson family of 'statesmen' farmers lived at Nab Cottage, separated from the shores of Rydal Water by the modern A591 road, and sited below Nab Scar. This is a traditional farmhouse, dating from 1702, and is in private ownership. De Quincey lived with the Simpsons at Nab Cottage for a time prior to his marriage to Margaret Simpson, and in 1829 he took on the mortgage when Margaret's father, John, got into debt. It is not surprising in view of de Quincey's habitually parlous financial state that he was forced to sell the house in 1833, having occupied it from time to time during the previous four years. It was bought by the major local landowning family of Le Fleming, and later rented to Hartley Coleridge.

Fox Ghyll is located off a minor road which runs through Under Loughrigg from Ambleside to a junction with the A591 at Pelter Bridge, Rydal. Dorothy Wordsworth often used this road between Grasmere and Ambleside, and close to Fox Ghyll is Fox How, built as a holiday home in 1833 by the famous Rugby School headmaster Dr Thomas Arnold, and later associated with his son, the poet Matthew Arnold.

De Quincey rented Fox Ghyll – in the shadow of Loughrigg Fell – from 1820, intending to stay for just six months, but the family retained the house until 1825, when they were evicted by its new owner Letitia Luff, a friend of Dorothy Wordsworth. The house was greatly extended and the gardens landscaped under Luff's ownership.

Hartley Coleridge
(1796–1849)

David Hartley Coleridge was the eldest son of
Samuel Taylor Coleridge, who named him after the
physician-theologian David Hartley. He was born
in the West Country, but when he was four years
old the family moved to Greta Hall in Keswick, so
Hartley grew up in the Lake District.

He was, by all accounts, a strange child,
old beyond his years and possessed of a vivid
imagination. He had great intellectual precocity.
At a very young age he is supposed to have told
his father, 'The pity is, I'se always thinking
of my thoughts.' This did not trouble his
father, and he wrote 'Hartley is considered a
genius by Wordsworth and Southey, indeed by
everyone who has seen much of him.' The boy's
development did, however, trouble Wordsworth and
Southey, who became responsible for Hartley's
education and welfare, most notably when he
was sent to school in Ambleside, and lodged
with the Wordsworth family during term time.
Wordsworth's concerns appear in his poem
To H. C. Six Years Old, in which he writes:

Water Lilies
Water lilies on Brothers Water. Dorothy Wordsworth referred to
it as 'the glittering lively lake'.

O blessed vision! happy child!
Thou art so exquisitely wild,
I think of thee with many fears
For what may be thy lot in future years.

Hartley was also the subject of two of his father's best-known poems, *Frost At Midnight* and *The Nightingale*, and he is also referred to in the conclusion to the second part of *Christabel*. 'A fairy thing with red round cheeks/That always finds and never seeks ...'

Hartley and his younger brother, Derwent, both attended school in Ambleside, but as Derwent was later to write, '... he was educated – by desultory reading, by the living voice of Coleridge, Southey and Wordsworth, Lloyd, Wilson and de Quincey – and, again, by homely familiarity with the town's folk and country folk of every degree; lastly by recurring hours of solitude – with lonely wanderings with the murmur of the Brathay in his ear.'

Hartley inherited his father's conversational powers and some of his intellect, and in 1814 went up to Merton College at Oxford, where he was a very good student, and first seriously began to write poetry. Always concerned that he was unattractive to women, partly owing to his lack of height, Hartley became convinced that winning the Newdigate Prize – the university's prestigious annual verse award – would improve his chances with the opposite sex, and his failure to do so partly explains his descent into excessive drinking.

Nonetheless, Hartley Coleridge ultimately was elected a fellow of Oriel College, but his intemperate habits during his probationary year brought his academic career to a close, and he proceeded to live in Gray's Inn in London for two years, contributing some notable sonnets to the *London Magazine* during his time there. The call of the Lakes was strong, however, and he returned to Westmorland, partly owing to a feeling of nostalgia for the place where he had grown up, and partly because he felt he would be less likely to succumb to insobriety away from the influences of Oxford or London society. In this, he was sadly mistaken.

Hartley lodged in the hamlet of Clappersgate, near Ambleside, and taught at his old school in Ambleside for some five years until the establishment was forced to close. In Town End, Grasmere, Hartley lived at Rose Cottage from 1829 until 1840, when he moved to Nab Cottage on the shores of Rydal Water, where he remained for the final eight years of his life. Here he wrote some of his finest sonnets. At The Nab he lodged with the Richardsons, who found him '... as manashable as a bairn,' and in a sense he remained a child all his life, lacking the ability to concentrate for prolonged creative effort.

In 1833, he published *Poems, Songs & Sonnets*, and the sonnets in particular received much praise. In the same year his uncompleted *Biographia Borealis* appeared, being re-published three years later as *Worthies of Yorkshire & Lancashire*. He also contributed to the *London Magazine* and *Blackwood's* in Edinburgh.

Two observations exist of Hartley Coleridge during this period. In the first, he is described as ' ... a most strange looking mortal, a compound of eccentricity, immense power of reasoning and imagination, amiability, simplicity and utter want of self command.' In the second he is '... a little, round, high-shouldered man, shrunk into a little black coat, the features on his face moulded by habit into an expression of pleasantry and an appreciation of the exquisitely ludicrous ... He is very anxious to establish an Ugly Club and to be its chairman; but really he is quite unworthy of the station, for odd enough he is, but never ugly, there is such a radiant light of genius over all.'

The story of Hartley Coleridge is one common to many sons of famous people. Hartley always felt that he lived in the shadow of his father's greatness and he also had a sense of inferiority, wondering whether people accepted him because of who he was or for his own sake. That '... homely familiarity with the town's folk and country folk of every degree' during his formative years was to lead to an affectionate relationship with them later in life, and it was only among the people of Westmorland that he felt he was somebody as Hartley Coleridge, not Sam Coleridge's son. The locals loved him for his openness with them, his willingness and ability to talk to them as equals. Wordsworth noted, 'Everybody knows him, and everybody loves and takes care of him.' Canon Rawnsley makes clear in his *Reminiscences of Wordsworth Among the Peasantry of Westmorland* that the people took Hartley into their homes and hearts, quite literally into their homes on the many occasions when he went on lengthy drinking sessions, – '... pot-house wanderings' as Wordsworth described them. They considered him a greater poet than Wordsworth as a result of his sociability, and one old man expressed the popularly-held opinion that 'Hartley helped him (Wordsworth) a deal, ... did best part of his poems for him, so the sayin' is.' He was 'Li'le Hartley' to what Rawnsley calls the peasantry, and his lack of condescension contrasted favourably with Wordsworth, who always liked to keep the human subjects of his poems at arm's length. As one critic has written, 'Wordsworth asked the child questions; Hartley danced with her on the green.' One subject of Rawnsley's enquiries said of Wordsworth that '... folks goes a deal to see where he's interred; ... for my part I'd walk twice distance over Fells to see where Hartley lies.' In many ways, he was far more of a Lake Poet than either his father or Robert Southey, and certainly a truer 'Laker'.

Despite his naturalness with the local people, in private Hartley was a tortured soul, feeling that he could never live up to his father's expectations or his early promise, and feeling a profound unsuitability for the women's love he craved. He never married, though, as his poetry makes clear, he frequently loved from afar. This is a *motif* in many of his poems, which are frequently tinged with melancholy.

Rydal Water
Close to the house where Wordsworth lived for thirty-seven years.

Devoke Water
Lakeland's largest tarn.

The circumstances of Hartley's death in January 1849 are tragic yet somehow appropriate, for he contracted bronchitis as a result of spending a December night drunk in a ditch. He is buried in Grasmere churchyard, and when it came to the interment, Wordsworth — who loved Hartley dearly, and tolerated his shortcomings — said to the sexton, 'Let him lie by us; he would have wished it. Keep the ground for us — we are old people and it cannot be for long.' A year later, Wordsworth was buried close to Hartley, followed in turn by Dorothy and Mary.

Hartley once referred to himself as 'One of the small poets', a punning remark which, quite accurately, sums up his own view of his writing, as well as his stature. He did, however, excel as a writer of sonnets, his work being characterised by technical excellence, and he has been described as '... after Shakespeare our sweetest sonneteer.' The form suited Hartley, as he liked to compose a poem 'at one sitting'. He would frequently put at the foot of a page of composition a note to the effect of '... worth hammering at,' though he rarely did hammer. According to friends, he frequently wrote the first draft in as little as ten minutes, often knocking at the door of a cottage and begging paper and pencil when there was a poem in his head. He shared with Wordsworth a tendency to compose while walking, and described his method of composition in the following terms: '... I cannot foresee. Of all my verses, not a single copy was begun with any definite purpose. In every sonnet the idea has come upon me in the course of composition – sometimes it may be suggested by a rhyme – and yet if my own judgement be trustworthy, they are not deficient in singleness or completeness.'

The Selection

Dedicatory Sonnet, To S T Coleridge

Hartley Coleridge used this sonnet in dedicating his 1833 volume of poems to his father. Line three refers to his father's poem *Frost At Midnight* (*see* Coleridge).

Father, and Bard revered! to whom I owe,
Whate'er it be, my little art of numbers,
Thou, in thy night-watch o'er my cradled slumbers,
Didst meditate the verse that lives to shew,
(And long shall live, when we alike are low)
Thy prayer how ardent, and thy hope how strong,
That I should learn of Nature's self the song,
The lore which none but Nature's pupils know.

    The prayer was heard: I 'wander'd like a breeze,'
By mountain brooks and solitary meres,
And gather'd there the shapes and phantasies
Which, mixt with passions of my sadder years,
Compose this book. If good therein there be,
That good, my sire, I dedicate to thee.

Sonnet VI (Loved Thee Once ...)

From the 1833 'lifetime' edition of Hartley Coleridge's verse. Idealised, unattainable love is one of the most frequently recurring themes in Hartley Coleridge's poetry, which occasionally teeters on the brink of self-pity.

I loved thee once, when every thought of mine
Was hope and joy, – and now I love thee still,
In sorrow and despair: – a hopeless will
From its lone purpose never can decline.
I did not choose thee for my Valentine
By the blind omen of a merry season, –
'Twas not thy smile that brib'd my partial reason,
Tho' never maiden's smile was good as thine: –
Nor did I to thy goodness wed my heart,
Dreaming of soft delights and honied kisses,
Although thou wert complete in every part,
A stainless paradise of holy blisses:
I lov'd thee for the lovely soul thou art, –
Thou canst not change so true a love as this is.

Sonnet IX (Long Time A Child ...)

A beautifully-made sonnet, revealing of the way in which Hartley Coleridge viewed his own life.

Long time a child, and still a child, when years
Had painted manhood on my cheek, was I;
For yet I lived like one not born to die;
A thriftless prodigal of smiles and tears,
No hope I needed, and I knew no fears.
But sleep, though sweet, is only sleep, and waking,
I waked to sleep no more, at once o'ertaking
The vanguard of my age, with all arrears
Of duty on my back. Nor child, nor man,
Nor youth, nor sage, I find my head is grey,
For I have lost the race I never ran,
A rathe December blights my lagging May;
And still I am a child, tho' I be old,
Time is my debtor for my years untold.

Windermere (Winter)
Wordsworth was smitten by the view from Orrest Head and wrote about it.

Sonnet XV. To Wordsworth

Also from the 1833 edition, and the first of a number of poems written for Wordsworth.

There have been poets that in verse display
The elemental forms of human passions:
Poets have been, to whom the fickle fashions
And all the wilful humours of the day
Have furnish'd matter for a polish'd lay:
And many are the smooth elaborate tribe
Who, emulous of thee, the shape describe,
And fain would every shifting hue pourtray
Of restless Nature. But, thou mighty Seer!

'Tis thine to celebrate the thoughts that make
The life of souls, the truths for whose sweet sake
We to ourselves and to our God are dear.
Of Nature's inner shrine thou art the priest,
Where most she works when we perceive her least.

Sonnet XVI. November

Probably Hartley Coleridge's best-known poem. The month of November, with its connotations of death and the onset of winter in the natural world, is symbolic of the poet's prevailing feelings.

The mellow year is hasting to its close;
The little birds have almost sung their last,
Their small notes twitter in the dreary blast –
That shrill-piped harbinger of early snows:
The patient beauty of the scentless rose,
Oft with the Morn's hoar chrystal quaintly glass'd,
Hangs, a pale mourner for 'the summer past,
And makes a little summer where it grows:
In the chill sunbeam of the faint brief day
The dusky waters shudder as they shine,
The russet leaves obstruct the straggling way
Of oozy brooks, which no deep banks define,
And the gaunt woods, in ragged, scant array,
Wrap their old limbs with sombre ivy twine.

Sonnet XVIII. Night

From the 1833 edition. This poem has obvious echoes of *Frost At Midnight*.

The crackling embers on the hearth are dead;
The indoor note of industry is still;
The latch is fast; upon the window sill
The small birds wait not for their daily bread;
The voiceless flowers – how quietly they shed
Their nightly odours; – and the household rill,
Murmurs continuous dulcet sounds that fill

The vacant expectation, and the dread
Of listening night. And haply now she sleeps;
For all the garrulous noises of the air
Are hush'd in peace; the soft dew silent weeps,
Like hopeless lovers for a maid so fair –
Oh! that I were the happy dream that creeps
To her soft heart, to find my image there.

Time Was When I Could Weep ...

This piece first appeared in Derwent Coleridge's 1851 collection of his brother's previously unpublished poems. The poem is thought to refer to Dorothy Wordsworth in her old age.

Time was when I could weep; but now all care
Is gone – yet have I gazed 'till sense deceived
Almost assures me that her bosom heav'd;
And o'er those features – as the lightest air
On summer sea – Life play'd, did they but bear
One trace of Mind, faintly in sleep perceiv'd,
Wand'ring, from earthly impulse unreliev'd –
Through regions of Emotion, wild or fair.
Her mind is gone! and now, while over all
A ghastly dreaming quiet seems to lie,
All Sounds subdued to mournful harmony,
My heart is tranquil; sunk beyond the Call
Of Hope or Fear; and still must deeper fall,
Down-down with Time, till e'en remembrance die.

Full Well I Know

Also from the Derwent Coleridge edition. A poem about the burden of being the son of a great man.

Full well I know – my Friends – ye look on me
A living spectre of my Father dead –
Had I not borne his name, had I not fed
On him, as one leaf trembling on a tree,

A woeful waste had been my minstrelsy —
Yet have I sung of maidens newly wed
And I have wished that hearts too sharply bled
Should throb with less of pain, and heave more free
By my endeavour. Still alone I sit
Counting each thought as Miser counts a penny,
Wishing to spend my penny-worth of wit
On antic wheel of fortune 'like a Zany:
You love me for my sire, to you unknown,
Revere me for his sake, and love me for my own.

To Love - And Not Be Loved ...

From the 1851 edition; Hartley is in characteristic mood on the subject of love.

To love — and not be loved — is such my Fate?
Did God! — Oh! Could that gracious Sire create
A soul to feel and love his excellence
Yes — to adorn him with a faith intense
To love him in the earth and sky and sea,
Yet doom that soul to perish utterly?

I Have Been Cherish'd ...

This poem was published for the first time in 1942, having escaped Derwent Coleridge's 1851 edition, which consisted of as many of his brother's previously uncollected poems as he was able to collate. Compare with *Full Well I Know ...*

I have been cherish'd, and forgiven
    By many tender-hearted,
'Twas for the sake of one in Heaven
    Of him that is departed.

Because I bear my Father's name
    I am not quite despised,
My little legacy of fame
    I've not yet realised.

And yet if you should praise myself
    I'll tell you I had rather
You'd give your love to me, poor elf,
    Your praise to my great father.

He Lived Amidst Th'Untrodden Ways …

Hartley Coleridge in less reverential mood than when writing his other poems about Wordsworth. This is a satire on Wordsworth in the form of a parody of the 'Lucy' poem which opens 'She dwelt among the untrodden ways …', and shows the humorous, mischievous side of Hartley's personality that made him popular with so many people. When he discovered its existence, Derwent Coleridge managed to suppress the poem for fear of offending the ageing Wordsworth, and it did not appear until 1942. The 'Milk-white Doe' refers to Wordsworth's poem *The White Doe of Rylstone*.

He lived amidst th'untrodden ways
    To Rydal Lake that lead: –
A bard whom there were none to praise
    And very few to read.

Behind a cloud his mystic sense,
    Deep-hidden, who can spy?
Bright as the night, when not a star
    Is shining in the sky.

Unread his works – his 'Milk-white Doe'
    With dust is dark and dim;
It's still in Longman's shop, and Oh
    The difference to him!

Associated Places

Rose Cottage, where Hartley Coleridge lived from 1829 to 1840, is in private ownership, and is located in the hamlet of Town End, Grasmere, at the junction of the A591 and the minor road over White Moss which passes Dove Cottage.

From Rose Cottage, Hartley moved to Nab Cottage (*see* de Quincey) in 1840, and in that year he was visited by Branwell Brontë, brother to Charlotte,

Bilberries
The Buttermere Fells support the largest known area of bilberries in the Lake District.

Emily and Anne, and a man whose intemperate habits no doubt gave him a degree of common ground with his host. Brontë wrote to Hartley afterwards, 'You will, perhaps, have forgotten me, but it will be long before I forget my first conversation with a man of real intellect, in my first visit to the classic lakes of Westmorland.' While living at The Nab, Hartley Coleridge wrote many of his finest sonnets, and it was there that he received the last sacrament in the presence of Wordsworth in January 1849.

Grasmere churchyard (*see* Wordsworth).

Further Reading

Coleridge: Poetical Works – Oxford University Press
Encyclopaedia of Romanticism (Ed. Dabundo) – Routledge
De Quincey: Recollections of the Lakes and the Lake Poets – Penguin Books
English Romantic Poetry (Everest) – Open University Press
William Wordsworth: A Life (Gill) – Oxford University Press
The Illustrated Lake Poets (Lefebure) – W. H. Smith
A Literary Guide to the Lake District (Lindop) – Chatto and Windus
The Lakers (Nicholson) – Cicerone Press
William Wordsworth (Sands) – Pitkin Pictorials
Robert Southey: A Life (Storey) – Oxford University Press
Dorothy Wordsworth, Writer (Woof) – The Wordsworth Trust
The Grasmere Journals (Wordsworth, D.) – Oxford University Press
Guide to the Lakes (Wordsworth, W.) – Oxford University Press
Wordsworth: Poetical Works – Oxford University Press
Wordsworth: The Prelude – Penguin Books
English Romantic Verse (Ed. Wright) – Penguin Books
Romanticism: An Anthology (Ed. Wu) – Blackwell Publishers

Some Useful Websites

www.visitcumbria.com
www.lakedistrict-guide.co.uk
www.grasmere.com
www.wordsworthlakes.com
www.wordsworth.org.uk

www.rydalmount.co.uk
www.wordsworthhouse.org.uk
www.gretahall.net
www.hawksheadgrammar.org.uk